ATLAS
MODERN
WORLD
HISTORY

Editorial Advisers

Haydn Middleton
Derek Heater

Acknowledgements

Unit 2 Church Missionary Society (Archives G1 CH2/1892/66);
Unit 4 recto Mansell Collection;
Unit 4 verso Popperfoto;
Unit 5 The Metropolitan Museum of Art, Bequest of Seth Low, 1929;
Unit 7 Trustees of the Imperial War Museum;
Unit 10 (top) Novosti Press Agency; (bottom) Mary Evans Picture library;
Unit 11 © Solo Syndication;
Unit 12 Popperfoto;
Unit 13 BBC Hulton Picture Library;
Unit 14 Institute of Contemporary History and Wiener Library;
Unit 16 © Solo Syndication;
Unit 22 Popperfoto;
Unit 31 Visnews.

Illustrations (on Units 5,7,8,12,16,19,21, and 23)
by Oxford Illustrators.

© Oxford University Press 1989

©Maps copyright Oxford University Press

Oxford University Press Walton Street, Oxford OX2 6DP
Oxford New York Toronto
Delhi Bombay Calcutta Madras Karachi
Petaling Jaya Singapore Hong Kong Tokyo
Nairobi Dar es Salaam Cape Town Melbourne Auckland

and associated companies in
Berlin Ibadan

Oxford is a trade mark of Oxford University Press

ISBN 0 19 831660 7 (non net)   ISBN 0 19 831677 1 (hardback)

Printed in Hong Kong

Oxford University Press

Contents

Contents

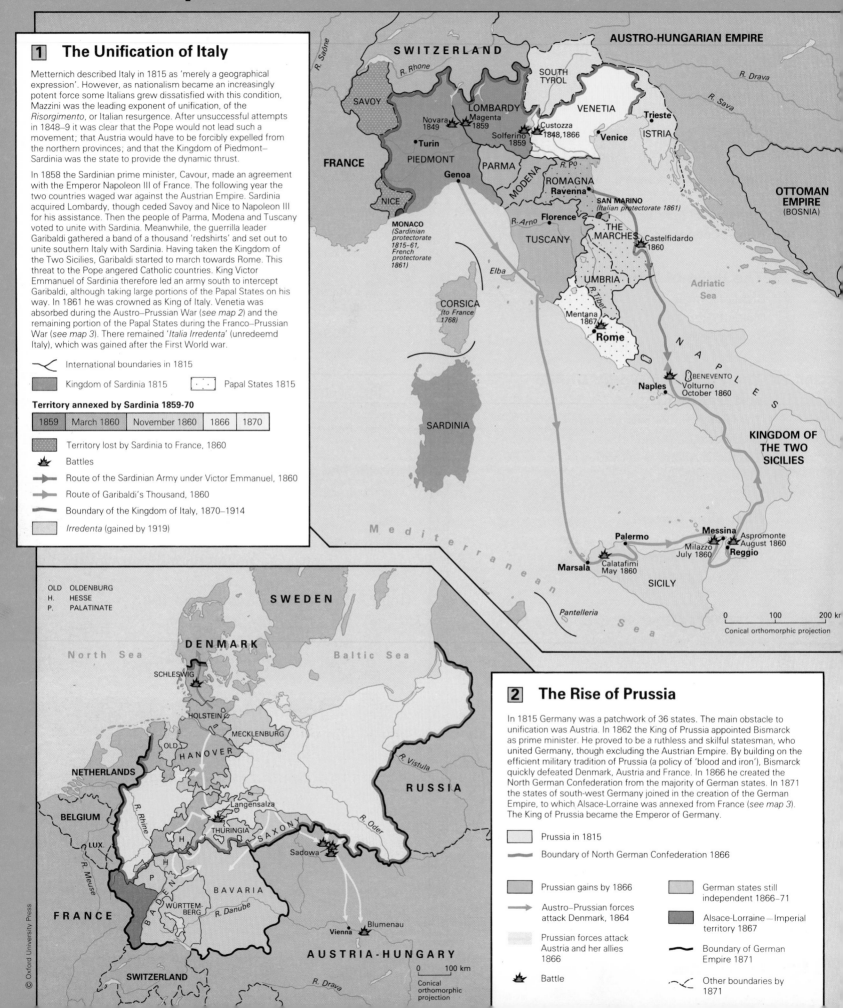

1 The Unification of Italy

Metternich described Italy in 1815 as 'merely a geographical expression'. However, as nationalism became an increasingly potent force some Italians grew dissatisfied with this condition, Mazzini was the leading exponent of unification, of the *Risorgimento*, or Italian resurgence. After unsuccessful attempts in 1848–9 it was clear that the Pope would not lead such a movement; that Austria would have to be forcibly expelled from the northern provinces; and that the Kingdom of Piedmont–Sardinia was the state to provide the dynamic thrust.

In 1858 the Sardinian prime minister, Cavour, made an agreement with the Emperor Napoleon III of France. The following year the two countries waged war against the Austrian Empire. Sardinia acquired Lombardy, though ceded Savoy and Nice to Napoleon III for his assistance. Then the people of Parma, Modena and Tuscany voted to unite with Sardinia. Meanwhile, the guerrilla leader Garibaldi gathered a band of a thousand 'redshirts' and set out to unite southern Italy with Sardinia. Having taken the Kingdom of the Two Sicilies, Garibaldi started to march towards Rome. This threat to the Pope angered Catholic countries. King Victor Emmanuel of Sardinia therefore led an army south to intercept Garibaldi, although taking large portions of the Papal States on his way. In 1861 he was crowned as King of Italy. Venetia was absorbed during the Austro–Prussian War (*see map 2*) and the remaining portion of the Papal States during the Franco–Prussian War (*see map 3*). There remained '*Italia Irredenta*' (unredeemd Italy), which was gained after the First World war.

- ⌇ International boundaries in 1815
- ▨ Kingdom of Sardinia 1815
- ⋯ Papal States 1815

Territory annexed by Sardinia 1859-70

1859	March 1860	November 1860	1866	1870

- ▨ Territory lost by Sardinia to France, 1860
- ✺ Battles
- → Route of the Sardinian Army under Victor Emmanuel, 1860
- → Route of Garibaldi's Thousand, 1860
- ⌇ Boundary of the Kingdom of Italy, 1870–1914
- ▨ *Irredenta* (gained by 1919)

2 The Rise of Prussia

In 1815 Germany was a patchwork of 36 states. The main obstacle to unification was Austria. In 1862 the King of Prussia appointed Bismarck as prime minister. He proved to be a ruthless and skilful statesman, who united Germany, though excluding the Austrian Empire. By building on the efficient military tradition of Prussia (a policy of 'blood and iron'), Bismarck quickly defeated Denmark, Austria and France. In 1866 he created the North German Confederation from the majority of German states. In 1871 the states of south-west Germany joined in the creation of the German Empire, to which Alsace-Lorraine was annexed from France (*see map 3*). The King of Prussia became the Emperor of Germany.

- ▨ Prussia in 1815
- ⌇ Boundary of North German Confederation 1866
- ▨ Prussian gains by 1866
- → Austro–Prussian forces attack Denmark, 1864
- ▨ Prussian forces attack Austria and her allies 1866
- ▨ German states still independent 1866–71
- ▨ Alsace-Lorraine —Imperial territory 1867
- ⌇ Boundary of German Empire 1871
- ✺ Battle
- ⌇ Other boundaries by 1871

OLD OLDENBURG
H. HESSE
P. PALATINATE

© Oxford University Press

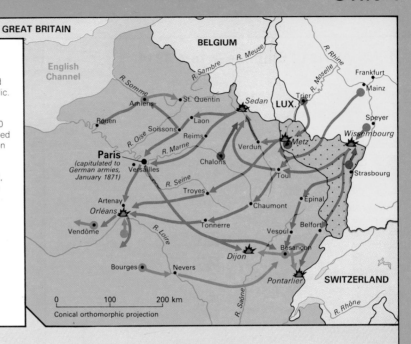

3 The Franco–Prussian War of 1870–1

In 1870 France was still generally considered the foremost military power in Europe—an idea cultivated by Napoleon III's myth that he had restored the grandeur of his uncle's Empire. Yet in this war she was defeated within half a year. The superior training and equipment of the Prussian army were clearly revealed. The first major battle was for the frontier fortress-town of Metz. The Germans forced the capitulation of the French army there. Striking north-west, the German army dealt a terrible blow at Sedan, where they not only forced the surrender of another French army, but captured the Emperor himself.

This humiliation led to the fall of the Second Empire and the creation of the Third Republic. However, the German armies were soon besieging Paris, an appalling ordeal for its citizens, which lasted from September 1870 to January 1871. The experience also aroused bitter social tensions, prompting the creation of the Commune, a communistic form of municipal government. The French government, now operating from Bordeaux, sued for peace. France lost Alsace-Lorraine and harboured feelings of resentment and humiliation and a desire for revenge.

France in 1870	German armies
German Empire 1870	French Imperial armies
Alsace-Lorraine – lost by France 1871, became Imperial territory of Germany	French Republican armies
	Battle
Other boundaries by 1871	Town

4 Europe's Population c. 1900

Throughout the nineteenth century the Industrial Revolution made rapid progress. Together there came an expansion of population and the concentration of workers in mining and industrial towns. It is estimated that the population of the continent increased during the century by over 120 percent. Manchester's rose from 77,000 to 544,000. The most densely occupied areas of Europe clearly reveal the impact of industrialization— the Midlands and North of England, Belgium, the Ruhr and Upper Silesia most especially. Nevertheless, in many states the bulk of the people worked on the land. Part of the explanation for these population trends must lie in the relationship between industrial and agricultural areas. The rapidly growing factory-towns sucked in labour from the countryside.

Population density (per square kilometre)

- More than 80 people
- 40–80 people
- 20–40 people
- 10–20 people
- Less than 10 people

International boundaries by 1914

Boundary between Austria and Hungary—one state but two separate monarchies

Imports and improving methods of food production prevented famine. Better health and sanitation also contributed.

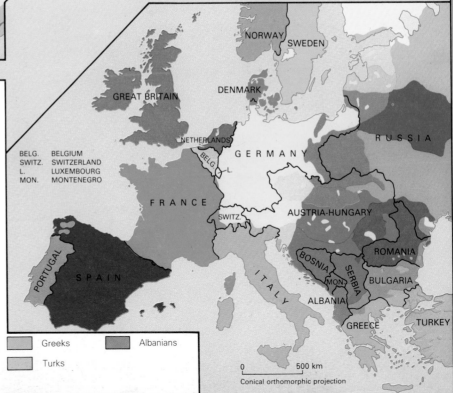

5 The Peoples of Europe

Nationality is a difficult idea to pin down. It has usually been equated with a sense of identity associated with language. The desire of a nation in this cultural sense to form their own nation-state was powerful in the nineteenth century. It led to the unification of Italy and Germany (maps 1 and 2). It also led to many demands for independence. Some of these, especially in the Balkans, were successful by about 1900. Others, like the Poles and Irish, had not yet achieved their aims. These demands for national independence were dangerous threats to the large European multi-national empires. The most variegated was that of Austria–Hungary, containing as it did, not just the dominant Germans and Magyars, but a number of sub-branches of the great Slav group of people.

British	French	Great Russians
Germans	Walloons	White Russians
Dutch	Spaniards	Ukrainians
Flemings	Portuguese	Poles
Danes	Italians	Czechs
Norwegians	Romanians	Slovaks
Swedes		Serbo-Croats
	Finns	Slovenes
Latvians	Estonians	Bulgars
Lithuanians	Magyars	

Greeks	Albanians
Turks	

BELG. BELGIUM
SWITZ. SWITZERLAND
L. LUXEMBOURG
MON. MONTENEGRO

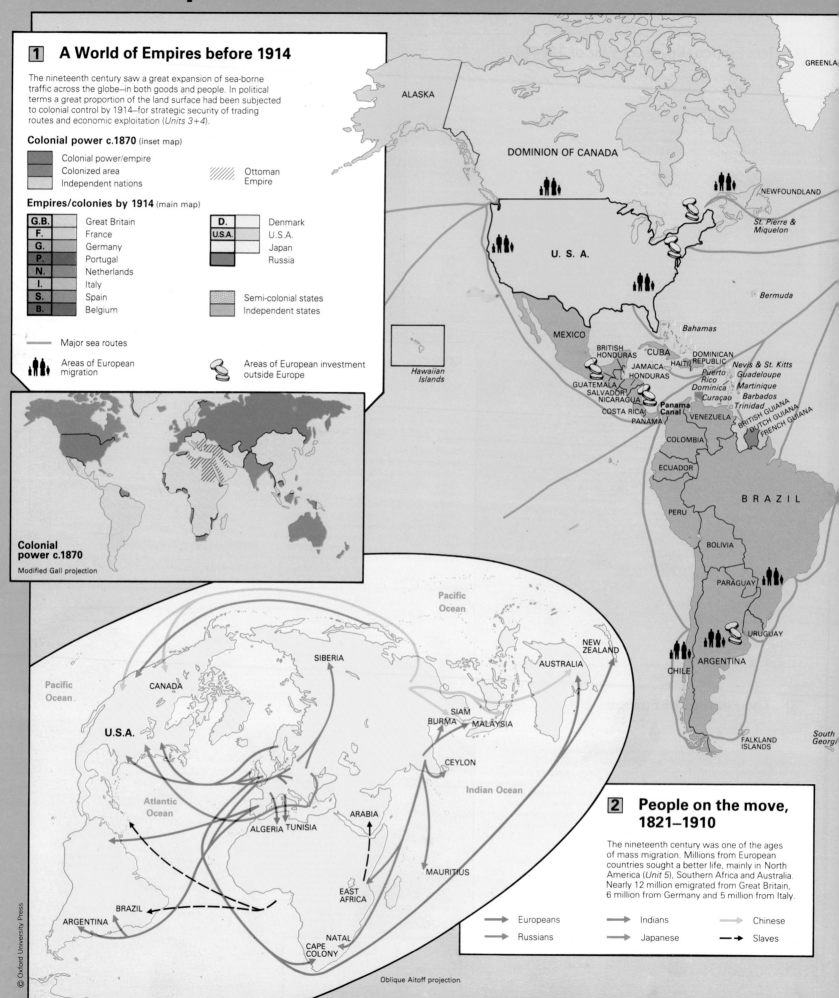

1 A World of Empires before 1914

The nineteenth century saw a great expansion of sea-borne traffic across the globe—in both goods and people. In political terms a great proportion of the land surface had been subjected to colonial control by 1914—for strategic security of trading routes and economic exploitation (*Units 3+4*).

Colonial power c.1870 (inset map)

	Colonial power/empire
	Colonized area
	Independent nations

/// Ottoman Empire

Empires/colonies by 1914 (main map)

G.B.	Great Britain
F.	France
G.	Germany
P.	Portugal
N.	Netherlands
I.	Italy
S.	Spain
B.	Belgium

D.	Denmark
U.S.A.	U.S.A.
	Japan
	Russia

Semi-colonial states
Independent states

Major sea routes

Areas of European migration

Areas of European investment outside Europe

Colonial power c.1870
Modified Gall projection

2 People on the move, 1821–1910

The nineteenth century was one of the ages of mass migration. Millions from European countries sought a better life, mainly in North America (*Unit 5*), Southern Africa and Australia. Nearly 12 million emigrated from Great Britain, 6 million from Germany and 5 million from Italy.

→ Europeans	→ Indians	→ Chinese
→ Russians	→ Japanese	--→ Slaves

Oblique Aitoff projection.

© Oxford University Press

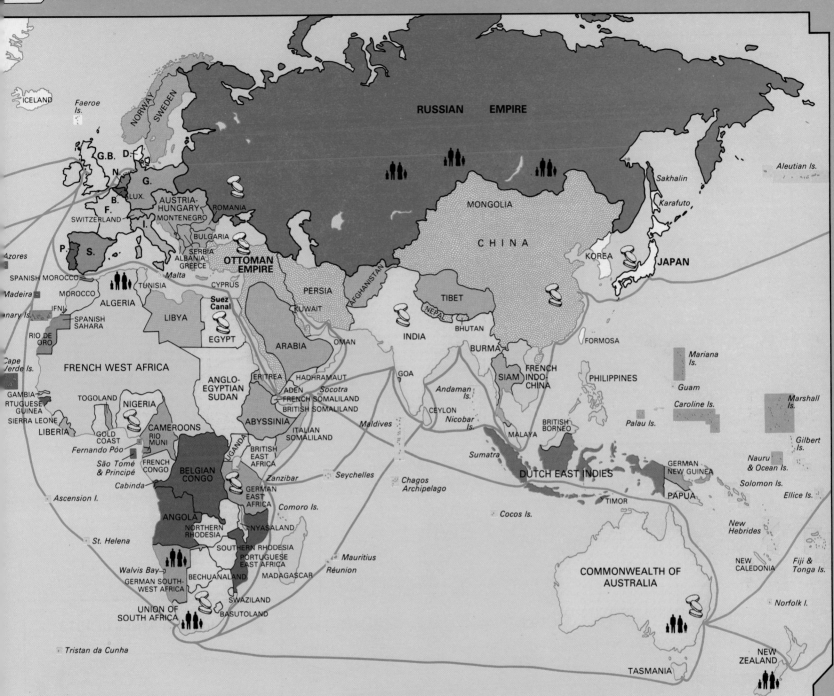

ICELAND
Faeroe Is.
NORWAY SWEDEN
RUSSIAN EMPIRE
Aleutian Is.
G.B. D.
N.
G.
Sakhalin
Karafuto
B. LUX.
F. AUSTRIA-HUNGARY
SWITZERLAND I.
ROMANIA
MONTENEGRO
MONGOLIA
KOREA
JAPAN
Azores
P. S.
BULGARIA
SERBIA
ALBANIA
GREECE
OTTOMAN EMPIRE
CHINA
SPANISH MOROCCO
Malta
CYPRUS
PERSIA
Madeira
MOROCCO
TUNISIA
AFGHANISTAN
TIBET
Canary Is.
ALGERIA
Suez Canal
KUWAIT
NEPAL
FORMOSA
IFNI
SPANISH SAHARA
LIBYA
EGYPT
ARABIA
OMAN
BHUTAN
INDIA
BURMA
RIO DE ORO
Cape Verde Is.
FRENCH WEST AFRICA
ANGLO-EGYPTIAN SUDAN
ERITREA
HADHRAMAUT
GOA
SIAM
FRENCH INDO-CHINA
PHILIPPINES
Mariana Is.
ADEN
Socotra
Andaman Is.
Guam
GAMBIA
PORTUGUESE GUINEA
SIERRA LEONE
LIBERIA
TOGOLAND
NIGERIA
GOLD COAST
CAMEROONS
FRENCH SOMALILAND
BRITISH SOMALILAND
ABYSSINIA
ITALIAN SOMALILAND
CEYLON
Nicobar Is.
Caroline Is.
Palau Is.
MALAYA
BRITISH BORNEO
Marshall Is.
Gilbert Is.
Fernando Póo
RIO MUNI
São Tomé & Príncipe
FRENCH CONGO
UGANDA
BRITISH EAST AFRICA
Maldives
Sumatra
GERMAN NEW GUINEA
Nauru & Ocean Is.
Solomon Is.
Ascension I.
BELGIAN CONGO
Cabinda
GERMAN EAST AFRICA
Zanzibar
Comoro Is.
Seychelles
Chagos Archipelago
DUTCH EAST INDIES
TIMOR
PAPUA
Ellice Is.
Cocos Is.
ANGOLA
NORTHERN RHODESIA
NYASALAND
SOUTHERN RHODESIA
PORTUGUESE EAST AFRICA
Mauritius
Réunion
New Hebrides
NEW CALEDONIA
Fiji & Tonga Is.
St. Helena
Walvis Bay
GERMAN SOUTH-WEST AFRICA
BECHUANALAND
MADAGASCAR
COMMONWEALTH OF AUSTRALIA
Norfolk I.
SWAZILAND
UNION OF SOUTH AFRICA
BASUTOLAND
NEW ZEALAND
Tristan da Cunha
TASMANIA

0   1000   2000 km
at the Equator
Modified Gall projection

Partition of the World in 1914

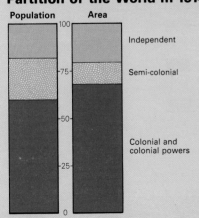

Population   Area
100
75
50
25
0
%

Independent
Semi-colonial
Colonial and colonial powers

When Europeans tried to impose their control and cultures on other lands, there was often, not surprisingly, fierce resentment. Uprisings took place in many areas of Africa and Asia. *Circa* 1900 there occurred the Holy War against the Dutch in Sumatra, the Mahdist uprising in the Sudan, the Ashanti War in the Gold Coast and the Boxer uprising in north-east China (*Unit 4*). Nowhere was this hostility more in evidence than among the Chinese, proud inheritors of an ancient civilization. This Chinese woodcut, made in the 1890s, depicts Christ as a pig being shot by arrows and his followers, the sheep, being decapitated.

Unit 3 Europeans in Africa

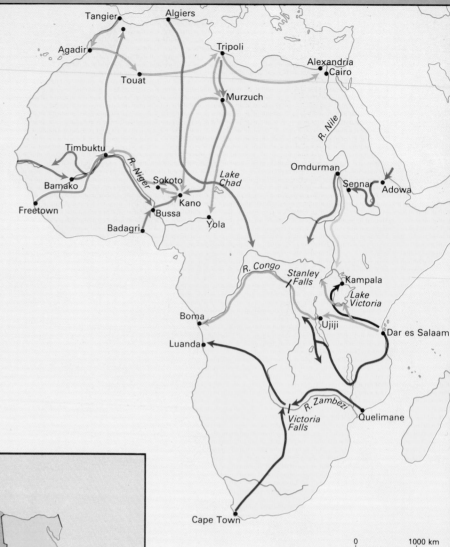

1 Routes of the explorers

Until the turn of the eighteenth century few Europeans penetrated into the interior of Africa. It was the unknown 'dark continent'. A few settlements dotted the coastline, those on the west mainly for the lucrative slave trade (Unit 2). Diseases like malaria and sleeping sickness deterred explorers. In the nineteenth century, however, an increasing number of Europeans ventured deep into the continent. Some were motivated by anthropological and geographical curiosity, some by Christian missionary zeal, others by a desire for wealth. Most shared an attitude of superiority over the peoples they considered 'uncivilized'. Nevertheless, they collected a great deal of information about the continent. The exploits of some, most notably the Scotsman David Livingstone, became famous and thus helped to spread public interest about Africa. However altruistic many of these explorers and missionaries might have been, they helped pave the way for European imperial expansion into the continent (map 2). For example, Stanley was employed by the Belgian King to open up the Congo.

→ 1769–72	Bruce	→ 1857–9	Burton and Speke
→ 1795–1806	Mungo Park	→ 1862	Baker
→ 1822–7	Clapperton	→ 1862–9	Rohlfs
→ 1827–9	Caillé	→ 1868–71	Schweinfurth
→ 1841–73	Livingstone	→ 1871–7	Stanley
→ 1850–56	Barth	→ 1898–1900	Foureau-Lamy

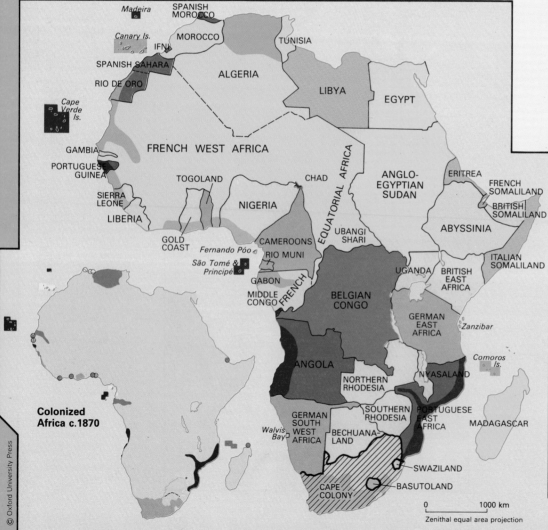

Colonized Africa c.1870

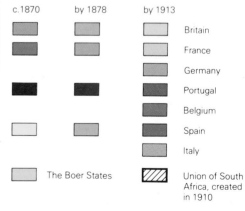

2 Colonized Africa in 1913

By c.1880 a number of European countries were laying claims to African territory in 'the scramble for Africa'. To prevent rival claims from degenerating into conflict, a conference of European states was held in Berlin, 1884–5, which recognized 'spheres of influence' as colonies. Within a generation virtually the whole continent was under European control.

Colonized areas

c.1870	by 1878	by 1913	
			Britain
			France
			Germany
			Portugal
			Belgium
			Spain
			Italy
		The Boer States	
		Union of South Africa, created in 1910	

0   1000 km
Zenithal equal area projection

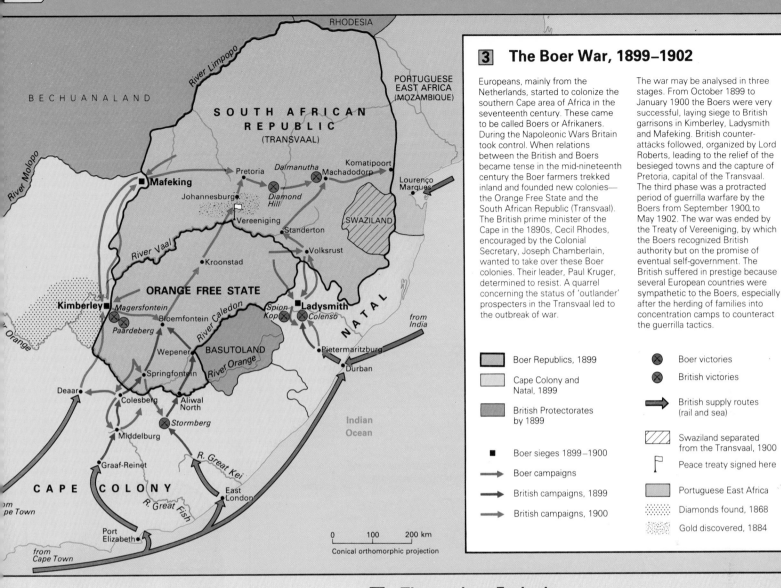

3 The Boer War, 1899–1902

Europeans, mainly from the Netherlands, started to colonize the southern Cape area of Africa in the seventeenth century. These came to be called Boers or Afrikaners. During the Napoleonic Wars Britain took control. When relations between the British and Boers became tense in the mid-nineteenth century the Boer farmers trekked inland and founded new colonies—the Orange Free State and the South African Republic (Transvaal). The British prime minister of the Cape in the 1890s, Cecil Rhodes, encouraged by the Colonial Secretary, Joseph Chamberlain, wanted to take over these Boer colonies. Their leader, Paul Kruger, determined to resist. A quarrel concerning the status of 'outlander' prospectors in the Transvaal led to the outbreak of war.

The war may be analysed in three stages. From October 1899 to January 1900 the Boers were very successful, laying siege to British garrisons in Kimberley, Ladysmith and Mafeking. British counter-attacks followed, organized by Lord Roberts, leading to the relief of the besieged towns and the capture of Pretoria, capital of the Transvaal. The third phase was a protracted period of guerrilla warfare by the Boers from September 1900 to May 1902. The war was ended by the Treaty of Vereeniging, by which the Boers recognized British authority but on the promise of eventual self-government. The British suffered in prestige because several European countries were sympathetic to the Boers, especially after the herding of families into concentration camps to counteract the guerrilla tactics.

▨ Boer Republics, 1899	⊗ Boer victories
▢ Cape Colony and Natal, 1899	⊗ British victories
▨ British Protectorates by 1899	→ British supply routes (rail and sea)
■ Boer sieges 1899–1900	▨ Swaziland separated from the Transvaal, 1900
→ Boer campaigns	⚑ Peace treaty signed here
→ British campaigns, 1899	▨ Portuguese East Africa
→ British campaigns, 1900	⠿ Diamonds found, 1868
	⣿ Gold discovered, 1884

0   100   200 km

Conical orthomorphic projection

4 The roads to Fashoda

Britain had an ambition for imperial control 'from the Cape to Cairo'; France, from the Atlantic coast to the Red Sea. In 1898 Major Marchand arrived at the derelict fort of Fashoda at the 'cross-roads' of these colonial drives and raised the French flag. A fortnight later, General Kitchener arrived, having defeated the Sudanese at the Battle of Omdurman. The British forces were far larger and Marchand was ordered by his government to withdraw, thus averting war between them.

Colonial territories and ambitions, 1898

▢ → British	
▨ → French	
▨ German	▨ Spanish
▨ Portuguese	▨ Italian
▨ Belgian	

5 The importance of Africa

Africa has for centuries been important to Europeans as a landmass lying across the routes to Asia. The early Portuguese settlements in Angola and Mozambique were established to assist these lengthy journeys. When the Suez Canal was opened the route distances were dramatically reduced. Thus the journey from England to Bombay was cut by over 4,000 miles. The continent has also been a rich source of food products like cocoa and nuts, metals such as copper and gold and precious products like diamonds.

Raw materials exported to Europe

- Gold—discovered 1884
- ◆ Diamonds—discovered 1868
- C Cotton
- R Rubber   V Vegetable oil

▢ European colonial powers with territory in Africa

→ Routes from Europe to India and Australia after 1870

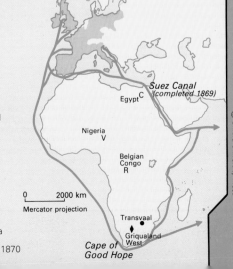

0   2000 km

Mercator projection

© Oxford University Press

0   1000 km

Zenithal equal area projection

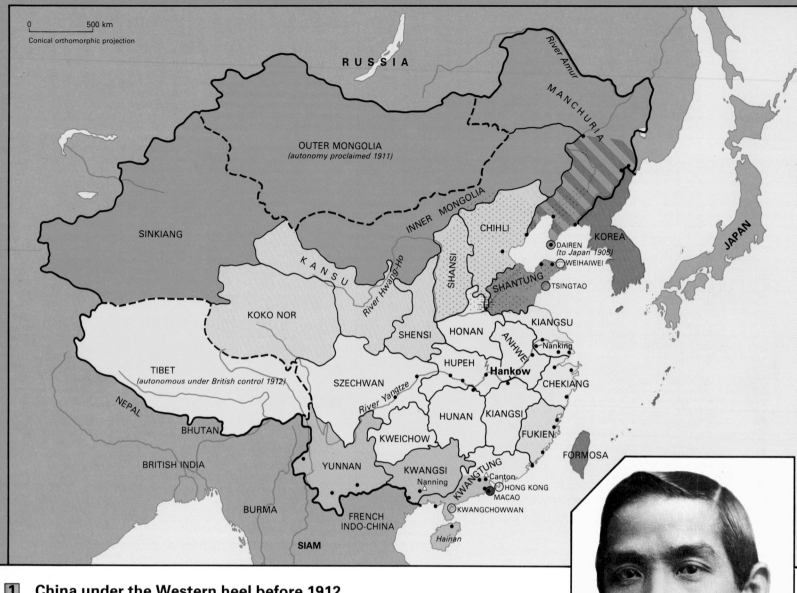

0   500 km

Conical orthomorphic projection

RUSSIA

OUTER MONGOLIA
(autonomy proclaimed 1911)

MANCHURIA

River Amur

INNER MONGOLIA

SINKIANG

CHIHLI

KOREA

⊙ DAIREN
(to Japan 1905)
◎ WEIHAIWEI

KANSU

River Hwang-Ho

SHANSI

SHANTUNG
⊙ TSINGTAO

KOKO NOR

SHENSI

HONAN

KIANGSU

ANHWEI

• Nanking

HUPEH

Hankow

TIBET
(autonomous under British control 1912)

SZECHWAN

River Yangtze

CHEKIANG

NEPAL

HUNAN

KIANGSI

BHUTAN

FUKIEN

BRITISH INDIA

YUNNAN

KWEICHOW

FORMOSA

KWANGSI

KWANGTUNG

• Canton

KWANGTUNG

△ Nanning

◉ HONG KONG
MACAO

◎ KWANGCHOWWAN

BURMA

FRENCH
INDO-CHINA

Hainan

SIAM

JAPAN

1 China under the Western heel before 1912

From the Opium War, which ended in 1842, China suffered a succession of humiliations. First the European colonial powers and Japan forced it, through a number of treaties, to open up its major ports to western trade. The failure of the anti-western Boxer Rising in 1900 led to China being carved up into European 'areas of influence'. China's traditional influence over neighbouring countries declined and some, like Burma (1886) and Indo-China (1885, 1893), fell under colonial rule. Formosa was lost to the Japanese in the war of 1894–5, and Russia occupied Manchuria in 1900.

Areas of influence, bases

 ○ British

⬛ ● Russian

⬛ ● German

⬜ ● French

⬜ Japanese

● Portuguese

▨ Russian occupation 1900–5

▨ Japanese acquisition

▨ Japanese occupation

 • Treaty ports and towns

Area of first Boxer activity

Main zone of Boxer Rising, 1898–1900

All this time, resistance to the ruling Manchu dynasty grew. The Taiping Rebellion of 1851–65 was the most serious uprising. Anti-Manchu secret societies became increasingly active. In 1905 Sun Yat-sen founded the T'ung Meng Hui which meant 'Revolutionary Alliance Party' and which inspired a major uprising in Hankow in 1911. By 1912 the Manchus had finally been overthrown and a republic proclaimed in Nanking. Fourteen years of unrest and confusion followed, during which Sun Yat-sen's Kuomintang (National People's Party) was formed (*Unit 11*).

△ Centres of anti-Manchu secret societies

⚡ Hankow flashpoint where the 'Double Tenth' revolution began on the tenth day of the tenth month, 1911

Province boundaries

International boundaries

Sun Yat-sen was a doctor who had been educated in Hawaii and Hong Kong. He was also a Christian. From 1895 he was in exile from China, preaching revolution against the Manchus and dodging the Chinese secret service.

When revolution broke out in 1911 he was in America. On his return he declared China to be a republic. His hope was that the new republic would be run on 'three principles'. These were:
a) nationalism (freedom)
b) people's rights (democracy)
c) the people's livelihood (which meant equal land rights).
Sun Yat-sen died in 1925.

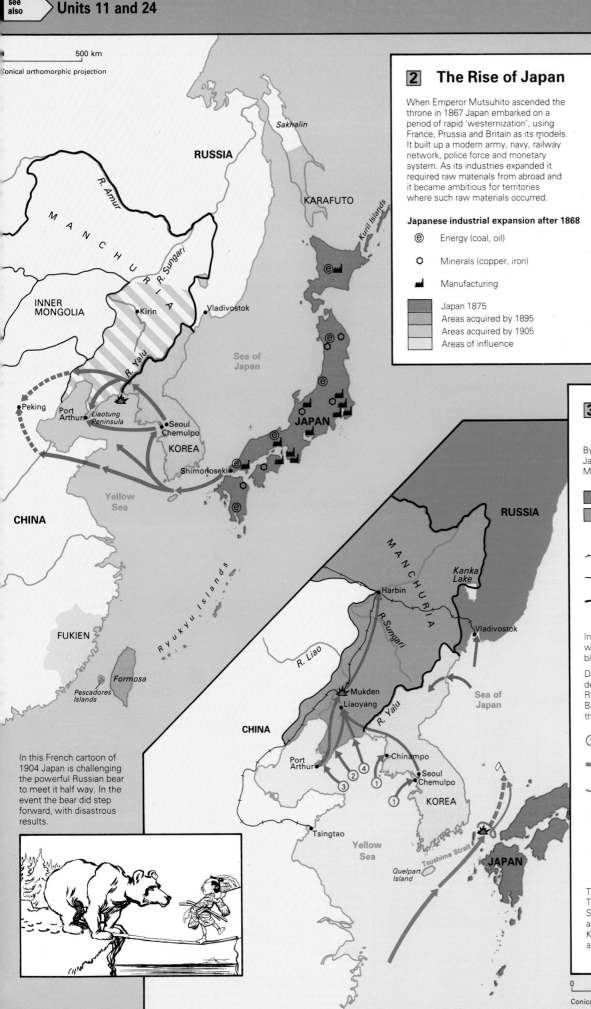

2 The Rise of Japan

When Emperor Mutsuhito ascended the throne in 1867 Japan embarked on a period of rapid 'westernization', using France, Prussia and Britain as its models. It built up a modern army, navy, railway network, police force and monetary system. As its industries expanded it required raw materials from abroad and it became ambitious for territories where such raw materials occurred.

In 1895 Japan defeated China and acquired Formosa and the Pescadores Islands under the Treaty of Shimonoseki. Victory over Tsarist Russia in 1905 (map 3) extended Japanese influence in Asia but also announced the emergence of Japan as a world power, provoking the interest of both the USA and Britain.

Japanese industrial expansion after 1868

- ⓔ Energy (coal, oil)
- ○ Minerals (copper, iron)
- 🏭 Manufacturing

- Japan 1875
- Areas acquired by 1895
- Areas acquired by 1905
- Areas of influence

Sino-Japanese War, 1894–5

- ➤ Japanese army movements
- ▪▪▪➤ Threatened 'pincer' movement on Peking, 1895
- 💥 Battle of Yalu River, 1894

- ∿ Chinese province boundaries
- — International boundaries

3 The Russo-Japanese War, 1904–5

By the beginning of the twentieth century Russia and Japan had become colonial rivals for Korea and Manchuria. War seemed inevitable.

- Russia
- Area of Russian influence 1904
- Japan
- Area of Japanese influence 1904

- ⊢⊣ Main railways, 1904
- ∿ Chinese province boundaries
- — International boundaries, 1904

In February 1904 the Japanese attacked Port Arthur without warning, sinking the Russian Pacific Fleet and blocking the harbour.

During the following year the Russians suffered several defeats on land as the Japanese advanced from the Yalu River to Mukden and, one major defeat at sea when its Baltic Fleet lost its flagship and three new battleships in the Tsushima Strait at the hands of Admiral Togo.

- ①➤ Movement of the four Japanese armies, 1904–5
- ➤ Movement of the Russian Baltic Fleet, 1905
- → Manoeuvres of the Japanese Fleet, 27 May 1905
- ⚐ Surrender of the remnants of the Russian Baltic Fleet, 28 May 1905
- 💥 Main battles: Mukden, 1905 Tsushima, 27 May 1905

The Russians were forced to negotiate, and at the Treaty of Portsmouth (1905) the Japanese acquired South Sakhalin (Karafuto), and the Liaotung Peninsula as well as extensive rights in Southern Manchuria. Korea became a Japanese Protectorate and was annexed in 1910.

In this French cartoon of 1904 Japan is challenging the powerful Russian bear to meet it half way. In the event the bear did step forward, with disastrous results.

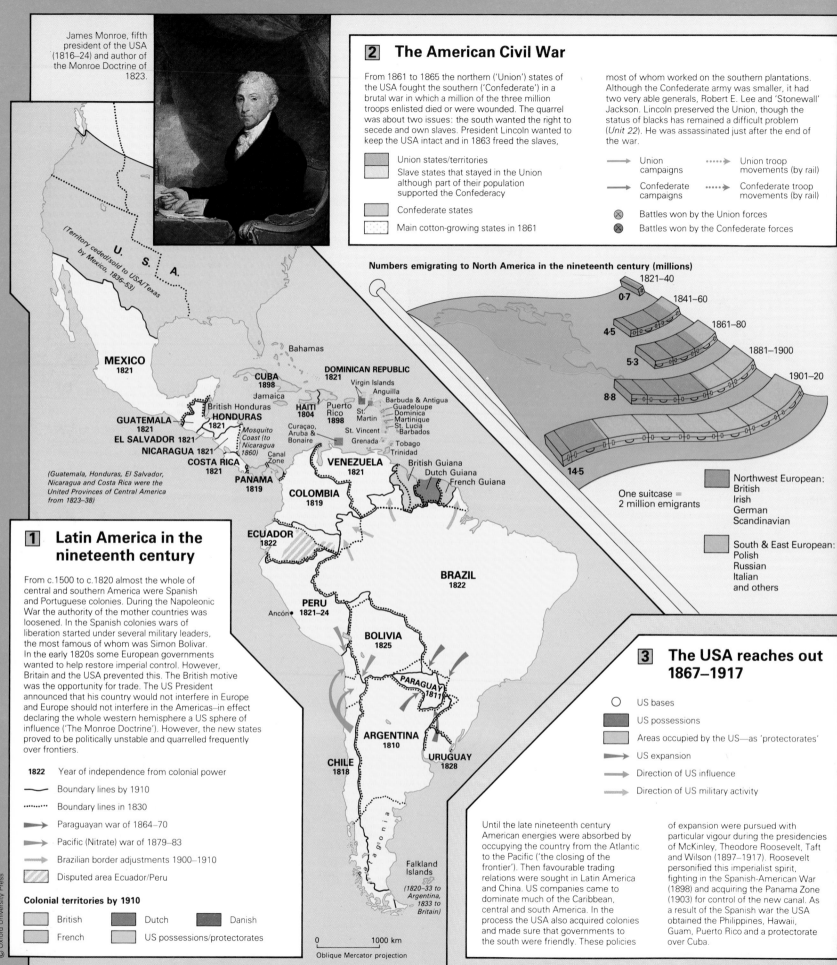

James Monroe, fifth president of the USA (1816–24) and author of the Monroe Doctrine of 1823.

2 The American Civil War

From 1861 to 1865 the northern ('Union') states of the USA fought the southern ('Confederate') in a brutal war in which a million of the three million troops enlisted died or were wounded. The quarrel was about two issues: the south wanted the right to secede and own slaves. President Lincoln wanted to keep the USA intact and in 1863 freed the slaves, most of whom worked on the southern plantations. Although the Confederate army was smaller, it had two very able generals, Robert E. Lee and 'Stonewall' Jackson. Lincoln preserved the Union, though the status of blacks has remained a difficult problem (*Unit 22*). He was assassinated just after the end of the war.

- Union states/territories
- Slave states that stayed in the Union although part of their population supported the Confederacy
- Confederate states
- Main cotton-growing states in 1861
- → Union campaigns
- → Confederate campaigns
- ⋯→ Union troop movements (by rail)
- ⋯→ Confederate troop movements (by rail)
- ⊗ Battles won by the Union forces
- ⊗ Battles won by the Confederate forces

Numbers emigrating to North America in the nineteenth century (millions)

Period	Millions
1821–40	0·7
1841–60	4·5
1861–80	5·3
1881–1900	8·8
1901–20	14·5

One suitcase = 2 million emigrants

- Northwest European: British, Irish, German, Scandinavian
- South & East European: Polish, Russian, Italian and others

Map labels

(Territory ceded/sold to USA/Texas by Mexico, 1836–53)

U.S.A.

MEXICO 1821

Bahamas

CUBA 1898
Jamaica
British Honduras
GUATEMALA 1821
HONDURAS 1821
EL SALVADOR 1821
NICARAGUA 1821
Mosquito Coast (to Nicaragua 1860)
COSTA RICA 1821
Canal Zone
PANAMA 1819

HAITI 1804
DOMINICAN REPUBLIC 1821
Virgin Islands
Anguilla
Barbuda & Antigua
Guadeloupe
Dominica
Martinique
St. Lucia
Barbados
Puerto Rico 1898
St. Martin
Curaçao, Aruba & Bonaire
St. Vincent
Grenada
Tobago
Trinidad

(Guatemala, Honduras, El Salvador, Nicaragua and Costa Rica were the United Provinces of Central America from 1823–38)

VENEZUELA 1821
British Guiana
Dutch Guiana
French Guiana
COLOMBIA 1819
ECUADOR 1822
BRAZIL 1822
PERU 1821–24
Ancón
BOLIVIA 1825
PARAGUAY 1811
ARGENTINA 1810
CHILE 1818
URUGUAY 1828
Patagonia

Falkland Islands
(1820–33 to Argentina, 1833 to Britain)

1 Latin America in the nineteenth century

From c.1500 to c.1820 almost the whole of central and southern America were Spanish and Portuguese colonies. During the Napoleonic War the authority of the mother countries was loosened. In the Spanish colonies wars of liberation started under several military leaders, the most famous of whom was Simon Bolivar. In the early 1820s some European governments wanted to help restore imperial control. However, Britain and the USA prevented this. The British motive was the opportunity for trade. The US President announced that his country would not interfere in Europe and Europe should not interfere in the Americas–in effect declaring the whole western hemisphere a US sphere of influence ('The Monroe Doctrine'). However, the new states proved to be politically unstable and quarrelled frequently over frontiers.

- **1822** Year of independence from colonial power
- —— Boundary lines by 1910
- ⋯⋯ Boundary lines in 1830
- ➤ Paraguayan war of 1864–70
- ➤ Pacific (Nitrate) war of 1879–83
- ➤ Brazilian border adjustments 1900–1910
- ▨ Disputed area Ecuador/Peru

Colonial territories by 1910

- British
- French
- Dutch
- US possessions/protectorates
- Danish

0   1000 km
Oblique Mercator projection

3 The USA reaches out 1867–1917

- ○ US bases
- ▪ US possessions
- ▪ Areas occupied by the US—as 'protectorates'
- ➤ US expansion
- → Direction of US influence
- → Direction of US military activity

Until the late nineteenth century American energies were absorbed by occupying the country from the Atlantic to the Pacific ('the closing of the frontier'). Then favourable trading relations were sought in Latin America and China. US companies came to dominate much of the Caribbean, central and south America. In the process the USA also acquired colonies and made sure that governments to the south were friendly. These policies of expansion were pursued with particular vigour during the presidencies of McKinley, Theodore Roosevelt, Taft and Wilson (1897–1917). Roosevelt personified this imperialist spirit, fighting in the Spanish-American War (1898) and acquiring the Panama Zone (1903) for control of the new canal. As a result of the Spanish war the USA obtained the Philippines, Hawaii, Guam, Puerto Rico and a protectorate over Cuba.

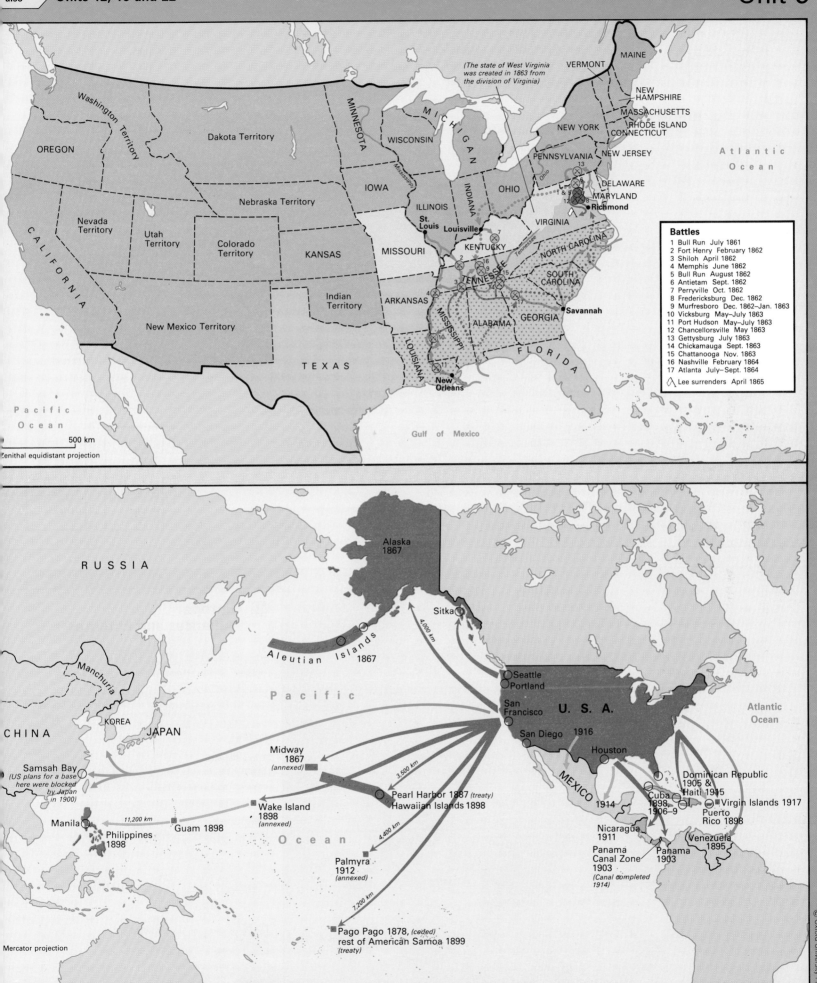

(The state of West Virginia was created in 1863 from the division of Virginia)

Battles
1 Bull Run July 1861
2 Fort Henry February 1862
3 Shiloh April 1862
4 Memphis June 1862
5 Bull Run August 1862
6 Antietam Sept. 1862
7 Perryville Oct. 1862
8 Fredericksburg Dec. 1862
9 Murfresboro Dec. 1862–Jan. 1863
10 Vicksburg May–July 1863
11 Port Hudson May–July 1863
12 Chancellorsville May 1863
13 Gettysburg July 1863
14 Chickamauga Sept. 1863
15 Chattanooga Nov. 1863
16 Nashville February 1864
17 Atlanta July–Sept. 1864

⋀ Lee surrenders April 1865

OREGON
Washington Territory
CALIFORNIA
Nevada Territory
Utah Territory
Colorado Territory
New Mexico Territory
Dakota Territory
Nebraska Territory
KANSAS
Indian Territory
TEXAS
MINNESOTA
WISCONSIN
IOWA
MISSOURI
ARKANSAS
LOUISIANA
MICHIGAN
ILLINOIS
INDIANA
OHIO
KENTUCKY
TENNESSEE
MISSISSIPPI
ALABAMA
GEORGIA
FLORIDA
VIRGINIA
NORTH CAROLINA
SOUTH CAROLINA
PENNSYLVANIA
NEW YORK
NEW JERSEY
DELAWARE
MARYLAND
VERMONT
MAINE
NEW HAMPSHIRE
MASSACHUSETTS
RHODE ISLAND
CONNECTICUT

St. Louis
Louisville
Richmond
Savannah
New Orleans

Mississippi
Ohio
Tennessee

Atlantic Ocean
Pacific Ocean
Gulf of Mexico

500 km
Zenithal equidistant projection

RUSSIA
Alaska 1867
Sitka
Aleutian Islands 1867
4,000 km

MANCHURIA
CHINA
KOREA
JAPAN

Samsah Bay
(US plans for a base here were blocked by Japan in 1900)

Manila
Philippines 1898
Guam 1898
11,200 km

Wake Island 1898 *(annexed)*

Midway 1867 *(annexed)*

Pearl Harbor 1887 *(treaty)*
Hawaiian Islands 1898

Palmyra 1912 *(annexed)*

Pago Pago 1878, *(ceded)*
rest of American Samoa 1899 *(treaty)*

Pacific Ocean

3,500 km
4,400 km
7,200 km

Seattle
Portland
San Francisco
San Diego
1916
Houston

U.S.A.

MEXICO
1914

Nicaragua 1911
Panama Canal Zone 1903
(Canal completed 1914)
Panama 1903

Cuba 1898, 1906–9
Puerto Rico 1898
Dominican Republic 1905 & Haiti 1915
Virgin Islands 1917
Venezuela 1895

Atlantic Ocean

Mercator projection

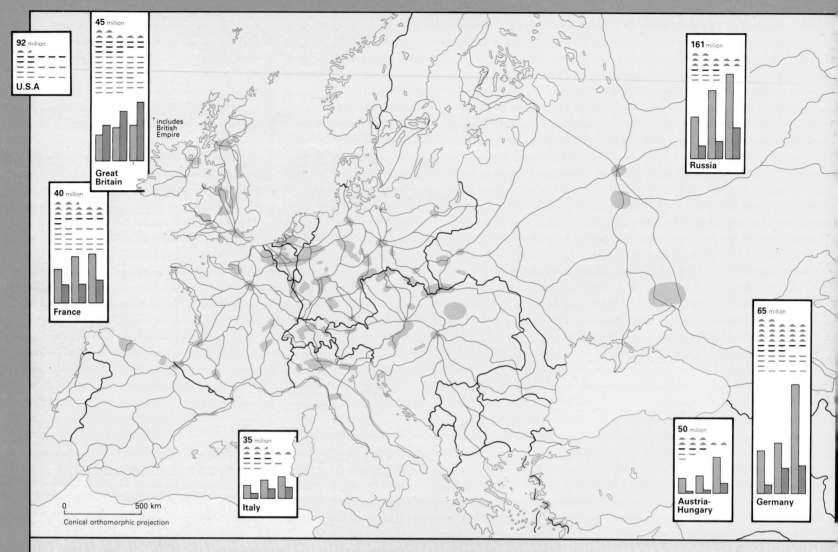

92 million

U.S.A

45 million

† includes British Empire

Great Britain

40 million

France

35 million

Italy

161 million

Russia

65 million

50 million

Austria-Hungary

Germany

0   500 km

Conical orthomorphic projection

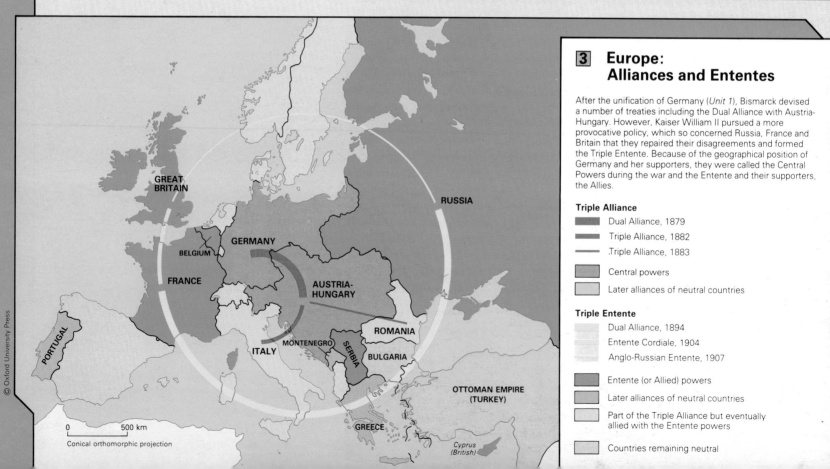

GREAT BRITAIN

RUSSIA

GERMANY

BELGIUM

FRANCE

AUSTRIA-HUNGARY

PORTUGAL

ROMANIA

ITALY

MONTENEGRO

SERBIA

BULGARIA

OTTOMAN EMPIRE (TURKEY)

GREECE

Cyprus (British)

0   500 km

Conical orthomorphic projection

© Oxford University Press

3 Europe: Alliances and Ententes

After the unification of Germany (*Unit 1*), Bismarck devised a number of treaties including the Dual Alliance with Austria-Hungary. However, Kaiser William II pursued a more provocative policy, which so concerned Russia, France and Britain that they repaired their disagreements and formed the Triple Entente. Because of the geographical position of Germany and her supporters, they were called the Central Powers during the war and the Entente and their supporters, the Allies.

Triple Alliance

- Dual Alliance, 1879
- Triple Alliance, 1882
- Triple Alliance, 1883

- Central powers
- Later alliances of neutral countries

Triple Entente

- Dual Alliance, 1894
- Entente Cordiale, 1904
- Anglo-Russian Entente, 1907

- Entente (or Allied) powers
- Later alliances of neutral countries
- Part of the Triple Alliance but eventually allied with the Entente powers
- Countries remaining neutral

1 Europe 1870–1914

From about 1870 tension rose and crises multiplied in Europe. One feature of the tension was the arms race: expenditure on armed forces increased dramatically from 1900. In particular, Britain and Germany competed to build a new generation of 'Dreadnought' battleships. Historians have debated whether the arms race heightened the tension by increasing fear or was merely a reflection of deeper economic and political rivalries.

― International boundaries, 1914

⟶ Railways

▭ Areas of greatest industrial activity

45 Population, 1914 (in millions)

Size of Army (January 1914)
▲ 100,000 soldiers

Size of Navy (by 1914)
— 5 battleships
— 5 cruisers
— 5 submarines

Military expenditure 1900–1914

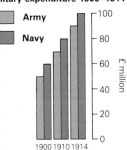
■ Army
■ Navy
(£ million)
1900 1910 1914

The most sensitive region was the Balkans (map 2). In a series of wars from 1817 to 1914 these small countries gained their independence from the Turkish Ottoman Empire. However, by the early years of the twentieth century the area was also the focus of Russian, German, Austrian and British ambitions and concerns; the source of many problems; and the location of the incident which led directly to world war. Russia befriended Serbia as a brotherly Slav nation. Germany developed commercial interests in the Ottoman Empire, started to build a railway from Berlin to Baghdad and was the ally of Austria-Hungary. Austria-Hungary was vulnerable as a multi-national empire in an age when nations wanted to form their own states. Britain was afraid that Russian influence might expand into the Mediterranean, endangering the route to India. After a war between Russia and the Ottoman Empire, frontiers were agreed for the independent Balkan states in 1878. Thirty years later Austria-Hungary annexed the Slav province of Bosnia-Herzegovina from the Ottoman Empire. Serbia protested. Russia supported Serbia. But Germany warned that she would join Austria-Hungary in the event of a war. 1912–13 there were two Balkan Wars, as a result of which the Ottoman Empire lost almost all its European territory and Serbia was enlarged. When, in July 1914, the Austrian Archduke Franz Ferdinand was assassinated by a Serbian at Sarajevo (⚡), the tension between the two states snapped. And because of suspicions, rivalries and alliances this local crisis escalated into world war.

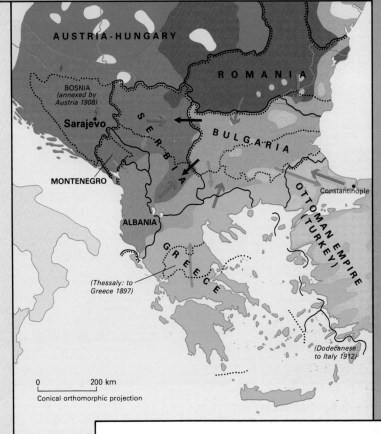

(Thessaly: to Greece 1897)

(Dodecanese: to Italy 1912)

0 ____ 200 km

Conical orthomorphic projection

2 The Balkans: flashpoint of Europe

·········· Boundaries after the Treaty of Berlin, 1878

―― Boundaries after the Balkan wars of 1912–13 (country names refer to 1913 areas)

Balkan War 1912
⟶ Balkan league attacks on Turkey

Balkan War 1913
⟶ Bulgarian attacks on Serbia

⟶ Counter-attacks by Serbia and her allies

▭ Serbs and Croats ⎫ Balkan
▭ Bulgars ⎬ Slavs
▭ Ukrainians
▭ Albanians
▭ Germans
▭ Hungarians   ▭ Greeks
▭ Romanians   ▭ Turks

4 The Schlieffen Plan

The Germans hoped for a speedy victory in the west to release troops for fighting against Russia. The plan entailed outflanking the main French defences by attacking through Belgium. The German army was then to encircle Paris and attack the French armies on the German frontier from the rear. The attack on Belgium violated a treaty which both Britain and Germany had signed. Britain therefore entered the war. French and British troops slowed down the German advance, thus foiling the Schlieffen Plan.

▭ Triple Alliance powers
▭ Dual Alliance powers
▭ Great Britain (expected to remain neutral)
―― International boundaries
⟝ Main railways

The Plan – Stage 1
⟶ German armies
⟹ French forces
⟶ Austrian forces

Stage 2
⟶ German forces
⟹ Slow to mobilize, Russian forces
⟶ Austrian forces

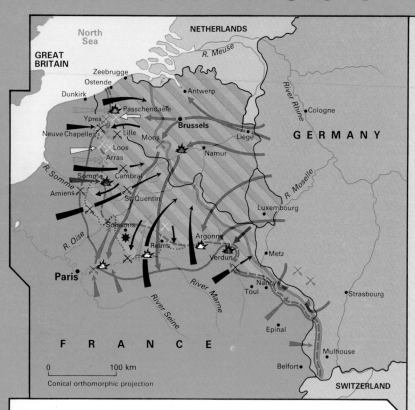

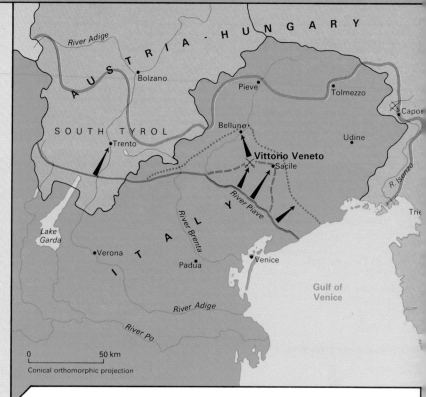

1 The Western Front

After the failure of the Germans to achieve a quick breakthrough (*Unit 6*), the war in the west reached a stalemate. Networks of trenches were dug, from which mass charges were made, resulting sometimes in the capture of a small stretch of land and almost invariably in horrendous casualties.

Even new technology in the form of poison gas and aircraft failed to break the deadlock, though the invention of the tank helped the Allies. The arrival of US troops finally gave the Allies superior strength. The generals have been criticised for callousness and incompetence for conducting campaigns with so much slaughter.

▨	Germany/Central powers
▨	Entente powers
⌇	International boundaries, August 1914

	Offensives		Battles	
	Central powers	Entente powers	with heavy losses	others
1914	➡	➡	✹	✕
1915	⇨	⇨		⊠
1916	➡	➡	✹	
1917	➡	➡	✹	✕
1918	➡	➡	✹	✕

——	Furthest German advance west, 1914
----	Trench line, November 1914 to March 1917
·······	Trench line by the summer of 1918
▬▬	Armistice line, 11 November 1918
▨	Area occupied by the Central powers, summer 1918
✹	French army mutiny, 1917

2 The Battle of Vittorio Veneto, 1918

Although Italy was a member of the Triple Alliance (*Unit 6*), she had a quarrel with Austria-Hungary: the Italian-speaking South Tyrol was part of the Austrian Empire (see *Unit 1*). Therefore, in 1915 Italy entered the war on the side of the Allies in the hope of gaining this region. Indecisive fighting took place in this mountainous terrain until the Battle of Caporetto in 1917 in which the Austrian and German troops decisively beat the Italians.

Reinforcements of British and French troops helped stem the advance of the Austrians and Germans as they pushed dangerously close to Venice. In October 1918 the Italians, strengthened by the appointment of a more able commander, engaged the Austrians, weakened by the redeployment of German troops to the Western Front. The ensuing Battle of Vittorio Veneto was a clear victory for the Italians, thus cleansing the shame of Caporetto.

▨	Central powers
▨	Entente powers
⌇	International boundaries, August 1914

Front line, 1918

——	24 October
----	30 October
·······	1 November
➤	Offensives of the Entente powers
✕	Battles
▬▬	Armistice line, 4 November 1918

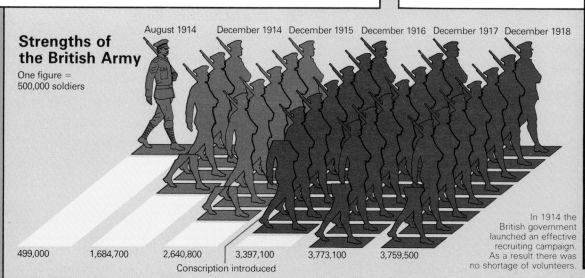

Strengths of the British Army

One figure = 500,000 soldiers

August 1914	December 1914	December 1915	December 1916	December 1917	December 1918
499,000	1,684,700	2,640,800	3,397,100	3,773,100	3,759,500

Conscription introduced

In 1914 the British government launched an effective recruiting campaign. As a result there was no shortage of volunteers.

THE VETERAN'S FAREWELL.

"Good Bye, my lad,
I only wish I were young enough
to go with you!"

ENLIST NOW!

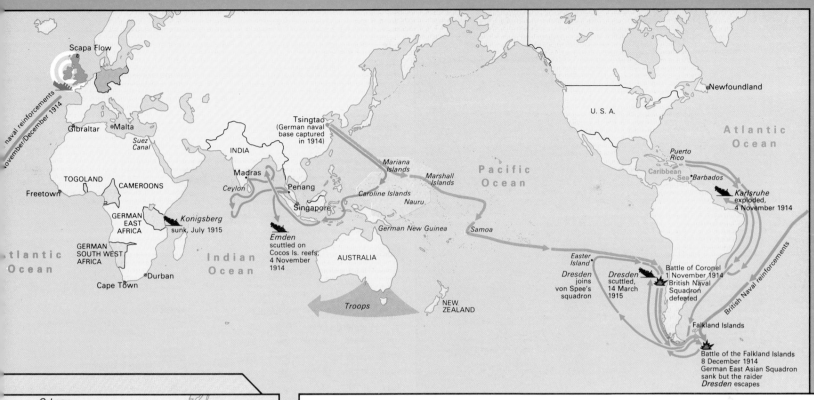

Modified conical orthomorphic projection

---

3 The War on the oceans

The German navy posed a threat to Britain's need to keep open her supply-routes. At first the greatest danger was a surface squadron commanded by Admiral von Spee in East Asia, and several 'surface raiders' at large in the Atlantic and Indian Oceans. However, after the sinking of merchant ships by the *Emden* in the Indian Ocean and the defeat of a British naval squadron at the Battle of Coronel, Spee's force was finally destroyed in the Battle of the Falkland Islands, and the raiders pursued and destroyed.

The Germans then concentrated on submarine warfare in the Atlantic in an attempt to shut off vital supplies of food to Britain from North America. By introducing the convoy system Britain managed to survive this peril. However, when a German submarine sank the passenger-liner *Lusitania* the victims included Americans. The USA entered the war.

	Great Britain
	British naval bases
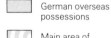	*Lusitania*, sunk 7 May 1915
	British Royal Navy
	Battle

	Germany
	German overseas possessions
	Main area of submarine (U-boat) activity after 1917
	German East Asia Squadron
	German 'surface raiders'

British merchant shipping losses

Agent	1914	1915	1916	1917	1918	Total
			(thousand tons)			
Submarines	1669	3326	886	749	5	6635
Mines	20	295	245	77	36	673
Surface ships	6	102	105	30	200	443
Aircraft	-	7	1	-	-	8
Total	1695	3730	1237	856	241	7759

German submarine losses

Agent	1914	1915	1916	Total
	(numbers of submarines)			
Patrol vessels	24	16	15	55
Mines	18	20	10	48
Convoy escorts	10	6	-	16
Decoy ships	-	6	5	11
Merchant ships	4	3	-	7
Men-of-war	1	-	2	3
Accidents	2	10	7	19
Unknowns	10	2	7	19
Total	69	63	46	178

---

4 The Battle of Jutland, 1916

British fleet
- Grand Fleet
- Second Squadron
- Battle cruisers

German fleet
- High Seas Fleet
- Battle cruisers

- Area of German submarine activity
- Minefield laid by the Germans
- Battle

Separated merely by the North Sea were two immensely powerful naval forces—the British Grand Fleet at Scapa Flow and the German High Seas Fleet at Wilhelmshaven. Neither side dared risk a major battle for fear of losing these great ships. However the two forces did engage off the Danish coast in 1916, the British under the command of Jellicoe and the Germans, Scheer. The British ships were of inferior design. Fourteen British ships were sunk to the Germans' eleven. Nevertheless, the German fleet retired to port for good, not daring to try to take control of the North Sea.

- Central powers
- Entente powers

Old battleships
Armoured cruisers
Battle cruisers
Light cruisers
Destroyers

Ships lost

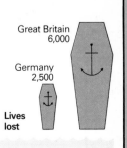

Great Britain 6,000

Germany 2,500

Lives lost

= 1 British ship (total tonnage lost = 112,000)   = 1 German ship (total tonnage lost = 61,000)

Unit 8 World War One 2

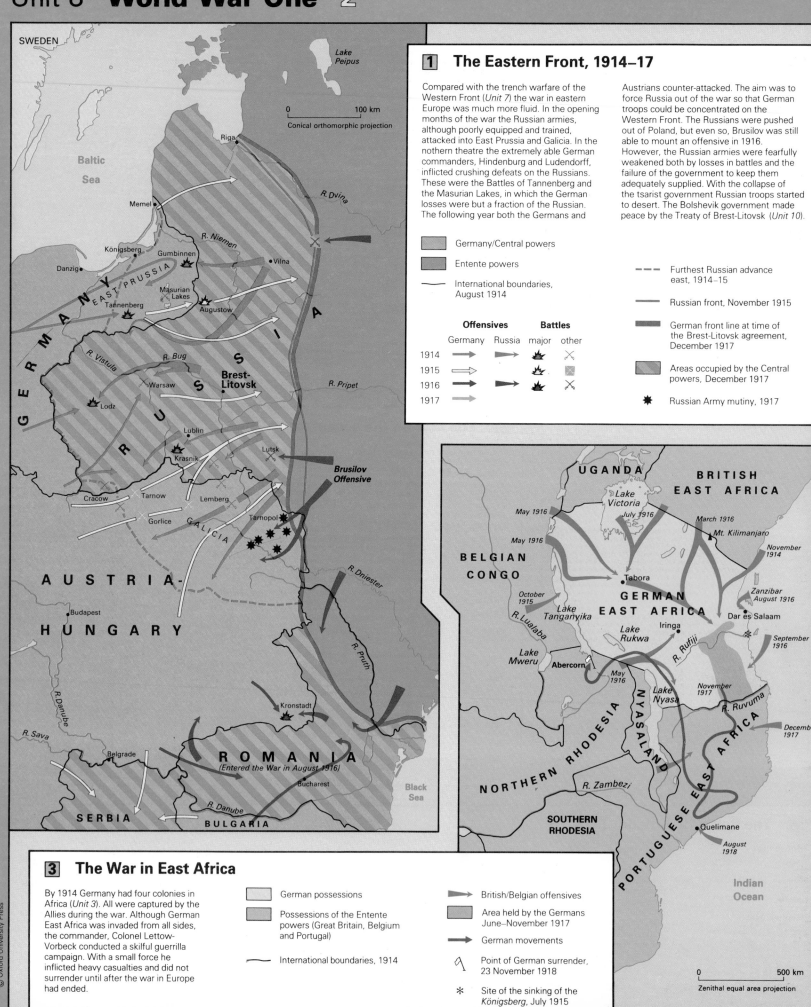

1 The Eastern Front, 1914–17

Compared with the trench warfare of the Western Front (*Unit 7*) the war in eastern Europe was much more fluid. In the opening months of the war the Russian armies, although poorly equipped and trained, attacked into East Prussia and Galicia. In the nothern theatre the extremely able German commanders, Hindenburg and Ludendorff, inflicted crushing defeats on the Russians. These were the Battles of Tannenberg and the Masurian Lakes, in which the German losses were but a fraction of the Russian. The following year both the Germans and the Austrians counter-attacked. The aim was to force Russia out of the war so that German troops could be concentrated on the Western Front. The Russians were pushed out of Poland, but even so, Brusilov was still able to mount an offensive in 1916. However, the Russian armies were fearfully weakened both by losses in battles and the failure of the government to keep them adequately supplied. With the collapse of the tsarist government Russian troops started to desert. The Bolshevik government made peace by the Treaty of Brest-Litovsk (*Unit 10*).

Germany/Central powers

Entente powers

International boundaries, August 1914

Furthest Russian advance east, 1914–15

Russian front, November 1915

German front line at time of the Brest-Litovsk agreement, December 1917

Areas occupied by the Central powers, December 1917

Russian Army mutiny, 1917

Offensives — Germany, Russia; **Battles** — major, other — 1914, 1915, 1916, 1917

3 The War in East Africa

By 1914 Germany had four colonies in Africa (*Unit 3*). All were captured by the Allies during the war. Although German East Africa was invaded from all sides, the commander, Colonel Lettow-Vorbeck conducted a skilful guerrilla campaign. With a small force he inflicted heavy casualties and did not surrender until after the war in Europe had ended.

German possessions

Possessions of the Entente powers (Great Britain, Belgium and Portugal)

International boundaries, 1914

British/Belgian offensives

Area held by the Germans June–November 1917

German movements

Point of German surrender, 23 November 1918

Site of the sinking of the *Königsberg*, July 1915

© Oxford University Press

2 The War in the Middle East

The Allies declared war on the Ottoman Empire in November 1914 after a naval incident provoked by the Germans. In Mesopotamia the British gradually advanced from the Persian Gulf, capturing Baghdad in 1917. In Arabia a revolt against Turkish rule was helped by the colourful British archaeologist-turned-soldier, T. E. Lawrence. And from Egypt a British army invaded Palestine.

However, the most famous campaign took place at Gallipoli in 1915. The idea was to try to take the Turkish capital of Constantinople. But the Turks pinned down the British, Australian and New Zealand troops with fire from higher ground. After suffering heavy losses, the Allied force was evacuated. Churchill, the First Lord of the Admiralty, who had supported the scheme, was forced to resign.

Central powers
Allies of Central powers
Entente powers
Allies of Entente powers

International boundaries, August 1914
Advances of Central powers
Advances of Entente powers
Front line ——— 1917 ——— 1918
Area of Arab revolt against the Ottoman rule

Gallipoli campaign: Turkish defences
Searchlights Main guns
Minefields Mobile guns

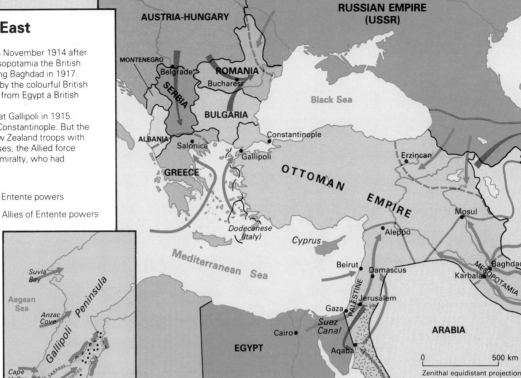

Military loss of life		
114,095		USA
335,000		Romania
325,000		Turkey
460,000		Italy
761,213		Great Britain
1,200,000		Austria/Hungary
1,358,000		France
1,700,000		Russia
2,000,000		Germany
446,000		Others including 251,900 British Empire

Civilian loss of life		
30,000		Belgium
800,000		Romania
812,296		Germany
1,000,000		Serbia/Austria
2,000,000*		Russia
100,000*		Sea/air raids
4,000,000		Massacre†
6,000,000*		Spanish influenza

Famine, disease and starvation

† Armenians, Jews, Syrians, Greeks
* at least

Relative losses in other wars		Per day
WW1	1914–1918	5509
American Civil War	1861–1865	518
Balkan	1912–1913	1941
Boer	1899–1901	10
Crimean	1854–1856	1075
Franco-Prussian	1870–1871	876
Napoleonic	1790–1815	233
Prusso-Austrian	1866	1125
Prusso-Danish	1864	22
Russo-Japanese	1904–1905	292

4 A Global Tragedy

At first the 1914–18 conflict was called 'the Great War'. It is now referred to as 'the First World War' to emphasise that both it and the war of 1939–45 (Units 17, 18 & 19) were global in scope. In all, twenty-five states participated and in addition troops from several combatants' colonies. The number of members of the armed forces killed and wounded exceeded that of the Second World War.

In addition, the First World War was waged as 'total' war. In many states the population and the economy were fully mobilized for the war effort. Furthermore, millions of civilians suffered death, injury and loss of homes as a direct or indirect result of the war. Revulsion against these horrors led to the over-optimistic belief that this was to be 'the War that will end War'.

International boundaries, August 1914
Central powers and allies
Entente powers and allies to 1917
Entente powers and allies at the end of the war

Nov. 1918 Dates of capitulation of German possessions

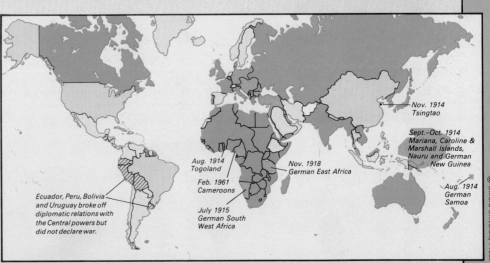

© Oxford University Press

3 The 'League against War'

The League of Nations was established with its headquarters in Switzerland, a country permanently neutral by international law. All member-countries sent representatives to the Assembly for debates, while decisions were made by a ten-member Council. However, the League was weak. It had no power of its own, except the will and strength of its members. And yet some of the powerful states were not members. The USA, preferring a policy of isolationism, did not join. The Communist government of the USSR would not join until 1934. Both Germany and Japan left in 1933 because they had no wish to be hamstrung in their aggressive policies. The weakness of the League in its attempt to prevent war was evident from its failure over the Abyssinian (*Unit 14*) and Manchurian (*Units 11 and 18*) wars.

By the eve of the Second World War it was moribund.
In addition to its attempted peace-keeping role, the League undertook several other tasks. It supervised the colonial administrations of former German and Turkish imperial possessions under the mandate system. It also performed valuable work of a social nature. The most effective was its International Labour Organisation, created to protect working people from exploitation.

■ Founder members	☐ Other members
⦂ Subsequent leavers with date of leaving	
■ Colonies of member states	■ Mandated territories
☐ Never members	✳ New war areas
+ Headquarters of League of Nations, Geneva	• Court of Justice, The Hague

Table of Mandates and Mandatory Powers

Mandates A (to be prepared for independence soon)

Iraq		Britain	
Palestine	under	Britain	formerly
Transjordan		Britain	Turkish
Syria and Lebanon		France	

Mandates B (to be prepared for eventual independence)

Cameroons		Britain	
Cameroun		France	
Togo	under	Britain	formerly
Togo		France	German
Tanganyika		Britain	
Ruanda-Urundi		Belgium	

Mandates C (no forseeable independence)

South West Africa		South Africa	
Western Samoa		New Zealand	
Nauru	under	Australia	formerly
New Guinea		Australia	German
Mariana, Caroline & Marshall Islands		Japan	

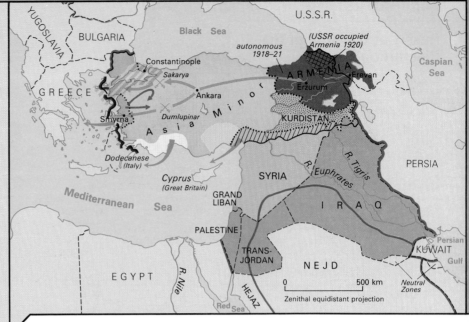

1 The New Europe

1919 statesmen assembled in Paris to work out the terms of a peace settlement. The dominant figure was Woodrow Wilson, the US President, partly because his own Fourteen Points provided the framework for the discussions. Wilson firmly believed that the war in Europe had been caused by the frustration of the desire for national self-determination. Consequently, he argued, if frontiers could be redrawn to coincide with the geographical distribution of nations, wars would be less likely. In practice, however, three problems inhibited the perfect implementation of this policy. One was the belief, held particularly by France, that Germany should be punished. Secondly, there was the problem of how to define a nation: in practice language was taken as the test. But most seriously there was the problem that nations were not distributed in coherent blocks, around which frontiers could be drawn. The creation of new nation-states was facilitated in eastern and central Europe by the collapse of the Habsburg and Romanov empires. Thus were born (or reborn) Czechoslovakia and Yugoslavia from Austria-Hungary, and Finland, Latvia, Lithuania and Estonia from Russia. Poland was reassembled from Russian, Austro-Hungarian and German territory. In addition transfers of land took place, including Transylvania and Bessarabia to Romania; Alsace-Lorraine to France; South Tyrol and Istria to Italy. However, in some border areas of mixed population the inhabitants were invited to vote in a plebiscite to determine their allocation. This method was used in Schleswig, East Prussia, Upper Silesia, Eupen-Malmédy and much later (1935) in the Saar. Nevertheless, in many countries national minorities were still present. An attempt was made to protect their interests by treaties guaranteed by the League of Nations (map 3).

- International boundaries, 1920
- Land lost by Germany
- Areas to be controlled by the League of Nations
- Demilitarized zones
- Plebiscite areas
- Land lost by Austria-Hungary
- Land lost by Russia
- Land lost by Bulgaria
- Land lost by the Ottoman Empire

POLAND New nation-states

2 After the Ottoman Empire

By the treaty of Sèvres all but Asia Minor and Constantinople were stripped from the former Ottoman Empire. Saudi Arabia became independent; but, much to the anger of the Arabs, other lands came under British and French control as mandates. After a war Turkey regained some lost land from Greece.

- —— Ottoman Empire, 1914
- ······ Turkey, 1920 after the Treaty of Sèvres

Occupation zones:
- Greek
- French
- Italian
- Demilitarized 'Straits' zone
- Plebiscite area

Mandates: British | French

Turkish-Greek War, 1920–22
- → Greek advances
- → Turkish advances
- ✕ Battles
- → Withdrawing occupation forces

Areas ceded by ▨ USSR ▨ France
- —— Turkey 1923, after the Peace of Lausanne

4 Germany made to pay for the War

The peace treaty with Germany, signed at Versailles, declared Germany guilty of causing the war. She was therefore punished in a number of ways. First, reparations were to be paid to compensate the Allies for deaths and damage. Secondly, all her colonies were seized. Also, to keep Germany weak she was forbidden to unite with Austria (a German-speaking country); to station troops in the Rhineland; to recruit anything but a small army; to build submarines or warplanes. The new government, which met at Weimar, was identified with this humiliation and was never very popular (Unit 14).

- —— International boundaries after Versailles, 1920
- Territory lost by Germany
- Demilitarized Rhineland zone
- Plebiscite areas which decided to leave Germany
- Plebiscite areas which decided to stay in Germany
- Areas controlled by the League of Nations
- ▰▰ Germany was forbidden to unite with Austria
- ⇨ Population movements out of Germany, 1918–19
- ⇨ Population movements into Germany, 1917–23

Reparations demands

	million goldmarks	method of payment
Early 1921	296,000	} 42 annual instalments
Late 1921	132,000	
1929	105,000	} 59 annual instalments
1930	34,000	
1932	53,000	
Actually paid	20,000	

	Germany Area (sq. km)	Population (millions)
1914	540,790	59
1921	467,300	68

© Oxford University Press

1 Russia at the time of the Revolution

By the standards of the other great European powers Russia was a backward country in 1917. Some industrialization was under way but about 80 per cent of the population were still peasants. The disruption of the First World War placed an impossible strain on the production and distribution of food, thus provoking discontent in both the major towns and in the armed forces. In February 1917 a revolution broke out. The Tsar abdicated and a Provisional Government was formed. Kerensky, the leader, tried to continue the war. But discontent remained and the Communist Bolsheviks carried out a second revolution in October. Their leader, Lenin, was determined to make peace with Germany. This was done by the Treaty of Brest-Litovsk. Although Russia lost much territory then, some of it was retrieved after the collapse of Germany.

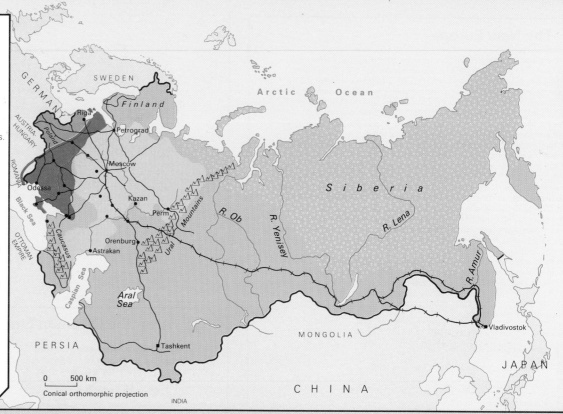

— Boundary of Russia, 1914

Area of permanently frozen subsoil (permafrost)

┼─┼ Trans-Siberian railway ── Other railways

─┼─ Armistice line, December 1917

Territory ceded to Central Powers by the Treaty of Brest-Litovsk, March 1918

Territory occupied by the Central Powers in 1918

• Towns where Bolsheviks took power, November–December 1918

Bolshevik-controlled territory by August, 1918

⟁ Mountains

4 The Birth of a European Revolution?

At the end of the First World War there was widespread fear among the governments and privileged classes in Europe of revolutionary upheaval. The experience of the war had itself fanned both social and political discontent. Furthermore, the Bolshevik revolution in Russia seemed to herald the start of widespread working-class rejection of established regimes. Marx had, after all, foretold the spread of revolution and appealed to working men of all countries to unite. In 1919 the Comintern (the Third Communist International) was established in Moscow to assist the work of the various Communist parties. And in practice from 1918 strikes of factory workers, mutinies of soldiers and sailors and urban riots and uprisings did take place in most European countries. Some of these demonstrations were in protest at Allied counter-revolutionary intervention in Russia.

However, in only two countries were there attempts at Communist revolution: in Germany and Hungary. At the end of the war the Kaiser was forced to abdicate. In the political confusion, while a new form of government was being consolidated, a group of Socialists led by Karl Liebknecht and Rosa Luxemburg and known as the Spartacists founded the German Communist Party. The following month (January 1919) an ill-prepared uprising occurred in Berlin. This was quickly suppressed by right-wing self-organized military units (*Freikorps*), who murdered Liebknecht and Luxemburg. In the meantime, a Bavarian Soviet Republic was declared in Munich. But it was brutally suppressed by the *Freikorps* after a period of virtual civil war.

The most nearly successful Communist revolution took place in Hungary. Here Béla Kun organized a Communist government, which lasted just over four months. His reforms, however, were marred by the cruelty of his supporters and his regime collapsed in the face of invasion by Romania.

⌒ International boundaries 1918–23

• Places where workers' and soldiers' councils were set up during November 1918

⚑ Violent suppression of communist uprising

⚑ Places where mass protests occurred against Allied intervention in Russia

➡ Red Army advances on Poland, June 1920

Germany, 1918

⚑ Places where the German Communist Party (Spartacus League) and left-wing radicals were in control

✗ Defeat of Red Army, August 1920

▨ Short-lived Soviet Republics established during 1919

"Have you volunteered to the Red Army?" - a political poster, 1920

2 The War with Poland, 1920–21

Poland had been extinguished as an independent state in 1795. After the First World War the Allies were determined to revive it. Because of the mixture of Poles and White Russians in the area it was difficult to define the eastern frontier. Lord Curzon set down the most appropriate boundary.

In November 1918 the new Republic of Poland came into existence with Pilsudski as its first president and the pianist Paderewski as prime minister. Poland immediately fought to gain extra land. In the war with the USSR the Poles penetrated as far as Kiev. The Russians counter-attacked and nearly took Warsaw. With French help the Poles established a new eastern frontier which incorporated many Russians.

	Poland by June 1920
⤳	Other international boundaries June 1920
⋯⋯⋯	Extent of Polish penetration into USSR by June 1920
▪▪▪▪	Curzon line, July 1920
⋯⋯⋯	Extent of Russian penetration into Poland by summer of 1920
💥	Battle for Warsaw (the 'Miracle of the Vistula'), August 1920
	Territory seized by Poland from Lithuania, October 1920
	Territory lost by USSR to Poland by the Treaty of Riga, 1921
⬡	Poland in 1921
—	Boundary of Russian Empire 1914
—	Soviet boundary, 1921

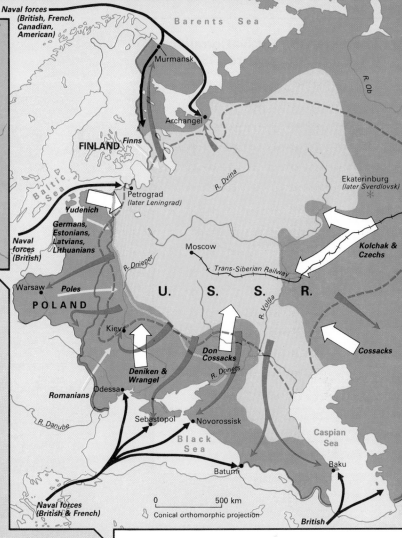

The Russian Revolution produced many posters of splendid design—an important means of communication in a barely literate society. Here a Bolshevik is displaying Lenin's three-fold promise: 'Power to the Soviets! Land to the peasants! Peace to peoples!' But a capitalist casts his sinister shadow over the revolutionary programme.

5 The USSR Encircled?

The Russian people throughout their history have experienced the utmost suffering from foreign invaders. Following the Civil War the Soviets saw themselves as encircled by hostile capitalist countries. Trotsky urged a policy of 'permanent revolution' to encourage the creation of Communist regimes in other countries. Stalin, however, favoured and put into practice 'Socialism in one country'—a policy of strengthening the USSR to withstand aggression.

Soviet Russia, March 1921

3 The Russian Civil War

Within days of the uprising in November 1917 the Bolsheviks controlled the government. However, their position was by no means secure. For example, while the royal family remained alive, they could be the focus of plots to restore the monarchy. They were all murdered.

More seriously for the Bolsheviks a number of counter-revolutionary 'White' armies were organized round the periphery of European Russia. By the summer of 1918 the Bolsheviks controlled only the central core of European Russia. Furthermore, the Allies in the First World War, both angry at Russia's withdrawal and fearing that the influence of Bolshevism would spread to other countries, also sent troops to support the Russian White armies.

However, by the autumn of 1920 the last White armies had withdrawn. The Bolsheviks were victorious in the civil war for several reasons. The commander of the Red Army was Trotsky, who proved to be a most skilful general. And although the revolutionaries were surrounded, their opponents were inefficient, utterly failing to co-ordinate their operations. Furthermore, the reform programme of the Bolsheviks was popular, consequently, the Whites received little support from the Russian people.

—	Boundary of Russian Empire, 1914
▬▬▬	Eastern front, March 1918 after the Treaty of Brest-Litovsk
	Area controlled by counter revolutionaries, August 1918
	Area controlled by Soviets, August 1918
⬜	'White' forces of Deniken and Kolchak
＊	Site of murder of Russian Royal Family, July 1918
➡	Forces of Western powers
⇥	Soviet area of control 1919, and counter-attacks 1920–1
➡	Other interventionist forces
—	Soviet territorial boundary, 1921

© Oxford University Press

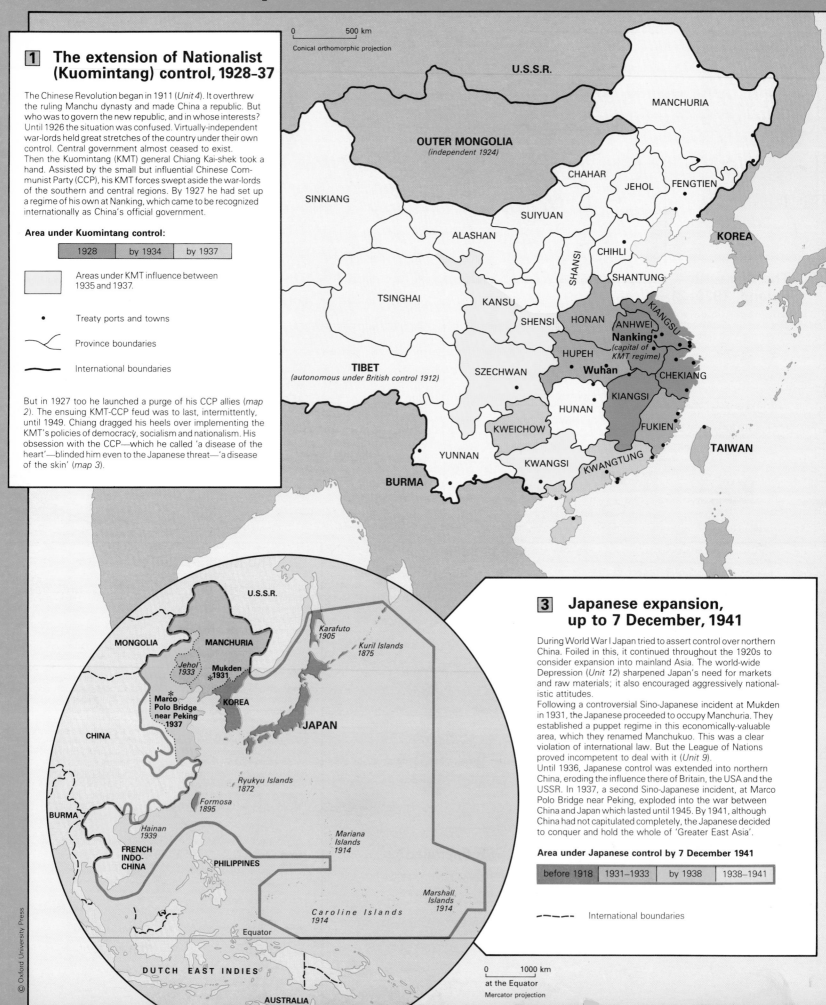

1 The extension of Nationalist (Kuomintang) control, 1928-37

The Chinese Revolution began in 1911 (*Unit 4*). It overthrew the ruling Manchu dynasty and made China a republic. But who was to govern the new republic, and in whose interests? Until 1926 the situation was confused. Virtually-independent war-lords held great stretches of the country under their own control. Central government almost ceased to exist.
Then the Kuomintang (KMT) general Chiang Kai-shek took a hand. Assisted by the small but influential Chinese Communist Party (CCP), his KMT forces swept aside the war-lords of the southern and central regions. By 1927 he had set up a regime of his own at Nanking, which came to be recognized internationally as China's official government.

Area under Kuomintang control:

1928	by 1934	by 1937

Areas under KMT influence between 1935 and 1937.

• Treaty ports and towns

⌇ Province boundaries

— International boundaries

But in 1927 too he launched a purge of his CCP allies (*map 2*). The ensuing KMT-CCP feud was to last, intermittently, until 1949. Chiang dragged his heels over implementing the KMT's policies of democracy, socialism and nationalism. His obsession with the CCP—which he called 'a disease of the heart'—blinded him even to the Japanese threat—'a disease of the skin' (*map 3*).

3 Japanese expansion, up to 7 December, 1941

During World War I Japan tried to assert control over northern China. Foiled in this, it continued throughout the 1920s to consider expansion into mainland Asia. The world-wide Depression (*Unit 12*) sharpened Japan's need for markets and raw materials; it also encouraged aggressively nationalistic attitudes.
Following a controversial Sino-Japanese incident at Mukden in 1931, the Japanese proceeded to occupy Manchuria. They established a puppet regime in this economically-valuable area, which they renamed Manchukuo. This was a clear violation of international law. But the League of Nations proved incompetent to deal with it (*Unit 9*).
Until 1936, Japanese control was extended into northern China, eroding the influence there of Britain, the USA and the USSR. In 1937, a second Sino-Japanese incident, at Marco Polo Bridge near Peking, exploded into the war between China and Japan which lasted until 1945. By 1941, although China had not capitulated completely, the Japanese decided to conquer and hold the whole of 'Greater East Asia'.

Area under Japanese control by 7 December 1941

before 1918	1931-1933	by 1938	1938-1941

- - - International boundaries

2 CCP fortunes until 1936

The Chinese Communist Party (CCP) was formed in obscure circumstances in the early 1920s. After the break with the KMT in 1927, its soviet base areas were subjected to Chiang's extermination campaigns. Mao Tse-tung's peasant-based soviet in southern Kiangsi survived from 1929 to 1934. Then he helped to organize its epic retreat into the north-west. This 'Long March' of at least 6,000 miles ended with the establishment of Mao's CCP headquarters at Yenan. Chiang was still determined to crush the CCP. But in 1936, threatened with deposition unless he formed a common front with the CCP against the Japanese, he agreed to postpone the struggle and a United Front was announced in 1937. But civil war was resumed after this 'Sino-Japanese War' of 1937–45 (*Unit 24*).

- ⬭ Original CCP soviet base areas
-〰 KMT lines of attempted encirclement
- ▬ The 'Long March' 1934–6
- ⤚ Main railways
- ▬ International boundaries

0 —— 500 km
Conical orthomorphic projection

MANCHURIA

CHAHAR
JEHOL   FENGTIEN

SUIYUAN
ALASHAN
CHIHLI
Yenan Soviet
SHANSI   SHANTUNG
KANSU   HONAN   KIANGSU
ANHWEI
SZECHWAN   HUPEH   CHEKIANG
KIANGSI
•Tsunyi   HUNAN   FUKIEN
KWEICHOW   Kiangsi-Hunan Soviet
YUNNAN   KWANGSI
KWANGTUNG
SHENSI
River Hwang-Ho
River Tatu
River Yangtze

An *Evening Standard* cartoon of 19 January 1933. It shows the Japanese in Manchuria trampling, unopposed, over the prostrate League of Nations. Meanwhile the British Foreign Secretary, Sir John Simon, is concerned only with saving the League's face.

Mercator projection

4 Japan's relations with major powers

The rest of the world could hardly ignore Japanese expansion. By 1937 the Fascist governments of Germany and Italy had joined Japan in an Anti-Comintern Pact. This was aimed against their common political rival—the USSR. A further agreement between them, the Tripartite Pact of 1940, had the objective of reordering Europe and the Far East. A year later, Japan signed a Non-aggression Pact with the USSR. This followed a Soviet victory over Japanese forces at Nomonhan in 1939. Henceforth, Japan's rear was secured, as it pursued its expansionist policies elsewhere in Asia. These policies, however, were a threat to the USA's considerable interests in the area. Relations between the USA and Japan had been deteriorating for some time. The Americans had been helping the Chinese in their war with Japan. Then, from 1939, they stepped up their economic pressure on the Japanese to withdraw. Japan anticipated an armed confrontation with the USA, and on 7 December 1941 it made a pre-emptive strike. By bombing the American naval base at Pearl Harbor, Hawaii, the Japanese effectively forced the USA into World War II (*Units 17 and 18*).

- ▬ Area under Japanese control by 7 December 1941
- • Headquarters of the League of Nations

U.S.S.R.
MONGOLIA
Nomonhan
*
CHINA
JAPAN
Hawaiian Islands

UNITED STATES

U.S.S.R.
GERMANY
Geneva•
ITALY

Japan's trading partners, 1918-22

◁ Exports
◁ Imports

G.B.
India   U.S.A
Other   China

© Oxford University Press

The world's banker

American loans abroad (1924–8) ($ million)

Annual totals:

Year	Amount
1924:	969
1925:	1076
1926:	1125
1927:	1337
1928:	1251
	5758 Total for period

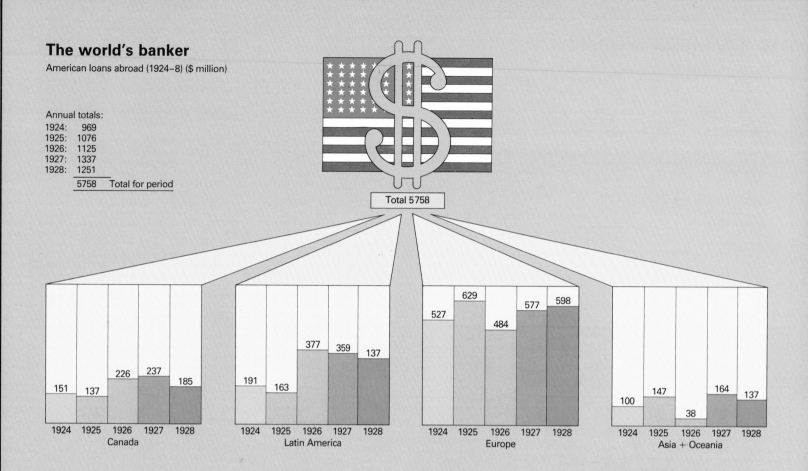

Total 5758

Canada

1924	1925	1926	1927	1928
151	137	226	237	185

Latin America

1924	1925	1926	1927	1928
191	163	377	359	137

Europe

1924	1925	1926	1927	1928
527	629	484	577	598

Asia + Oceania

1924	1925	1926	1927	1928
100	147	38	164	137

The affluent society

■ 1920   □ 1929

Registered cars

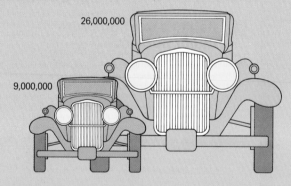

26,000,000

9,000,000

Radios in homes

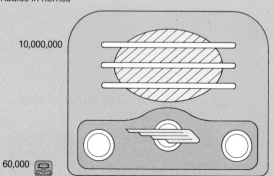

10,000,000

60,000

Many US cities, most notoriously Chicago and New York, were plagued by the violence of organized gangster mobs in the 1920s. Many innocent citizens were forced to pay for 'protection'. The police found prosecution difficult because the gangs so readily bribed or intimidated. Some, however, died in shoot-outs with police, as this photograph shows. It is of Arthur Flegenheimer, also known as 'Dutch' Schulz, who terrorized New York restaurant owners.

1 Presidential Elections, 1928 and 1932

Herbert Hoover, who won the 1928 Presidential election, was a distinguished international administrator and successful businessman. But when the US economy was rocked by the Wall Street Crash a year later, he could provide no solutions. Hence, the sharp reversal in his fortunes in the 1932 elections, when he faced the Democrat Roosevelt, who promised firm, confident and compassionate leadership. Roosevelt won in an unprecedented landslide.

In particular, Roosevelt believed that the state should play a far more active role than Hoover wished. The result was his New Deal programme. This involved using state funds (and running into deficit in the short term) to re-stimulate the economy. In this way, important public works could be undertaken and unemployment reduced. The graphs show how government spending increased substantially, though the numbers of unemployed remained obstinately high until absorbed by the massive manpower demands of the Second World War (*Units 17 and 18*).

1928

- ☐ Hoover (Republican)
  444 electoral votes
  21,392,190 popular votes

- ☐ Smith (Democrat)
  87 electoral votes
  15,016,443 popular votes

1932

- ☐ Hoover (Republican)
  59 electoral votes
  15,761,841 popular votes

- ☐ Roosevelt (Democrat)
  472 electoral votes
  22,821,857 popular votes

Figures on the map indicate numbers of electors per state

⌒ State boundary   ⌒ Boundary of the USA

Unemployment in the USA, 1829–40

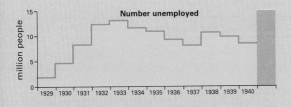

Number unemployed

million people

1929 1930 1931 1932 1933 1934 1935 1936 1937 1938 1939 1940

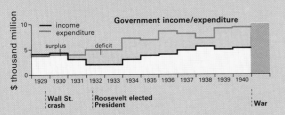

Government income/expenditure

— income
— expenditure

$ thousand million

surplus   deficit

1929 1930 1931 1932 1933 1934 1935 1936 1937 1938 1939 1940

Wall St. crash | Roosevelt elected President | War

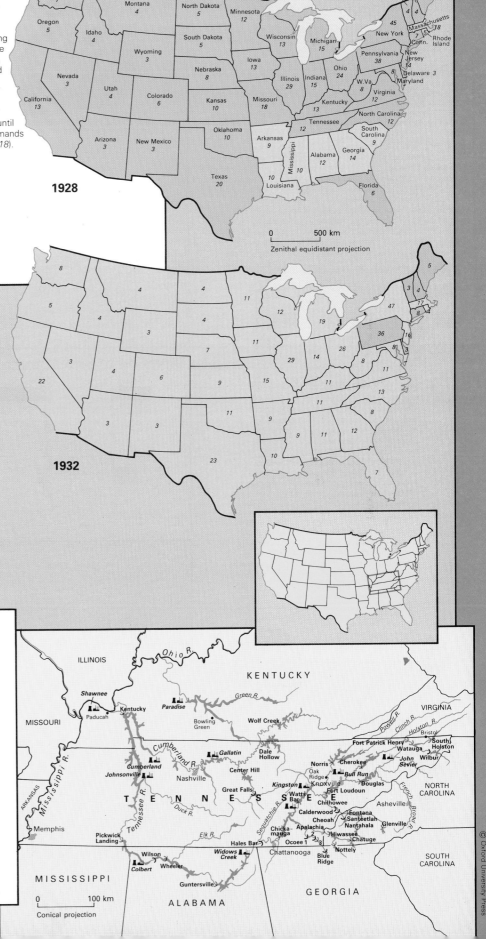

1928

0   500 km

Zenithal equidistant projection

1932

2 The Tennessee Valley Authority, 1933

The Tennessee Valley Authority (TVA) was the most impressive of the New Deal schemes and the most famous of the 'alphabet agencies'. Indeed, opponents of Roosevelt jeered at the proliferation of such government bodies as the CCC (Civilian Conservation Corps), the AAA (Agricultural Adjustment Association), the NRA (National Recovery Administration).

The great Tennessee Valley, an area equal to England and Scotland, was in a desperate condition. Constant flooding and soil erosion had reduced the farmers to the extremes of poverty. Roosevelt's scheme to restore the region was extraordinarily ambitious. That it succeeded was largely due to the ability and fortitude of the Lilienthal, one of the three Directors. As a result: dams were built; hydro-electric power-stations were constructed; land was restored to fertility; and new industries were created. But not only did the Tennessee Valley again become economically thriving. In the process of mobilizing local people in numerous co-operative enterprizes their enthusiasm was generated and their morale restored.

▬ Reservoirs

⌇ Dams in operation before 1933

⌇ Dams first in operation between 1933 and 1944

⌇ Dams first in operation since 1944

▰▰ Steam power plants

⌒ State boundaries

1 Britain and her World, 1931

In 1931 the British Empire and Commonwealth seemed a flourishing concern. It covered one-fifth of the planet's land-surface and embraced one fifth of its population. This empire 'upon which the sun never set' was composed of territories of extremely varied kinds. They varied in size, racial composition and amount of independence allowed for governing their own affairs. The most recently acquired members were the Mandates (*Unit 9*). They were lands taken from Germany and Turkey after the First World War and administered on behalf of the League of Nations. The most nearly independent were the Dominions, those countries with substantial white populations. Their right to virtually complete sovereignty was recognized by the Statute of Westminster in 1931.

In Britain there was still widespread pride at being the creator of this Empire. And among the educated elite there was pride too in contemplating the delicate task of gradually preparing these 'backward peoples' for political autonomy. The 'mother country' also benefited from her Empire in important tangible ways. Her international status as a major power depended on this imperial condition and the naval strength which accompanied this. Furthermore, Britain's fragile economic health depended significantly on her intra-imperial trading links, especially through the system of reduced tariffs known as 'Imperial preference'. There were nevertheless already signs of strain in the Empire, both in trading patterns and in mounting discontent in India.

- ▮ Great Britain and self-governing 'Dominions'
- ▮ British Indian Empire (British India and Indian Princely States)
- ▯ British colonies, dependencies of the 'Dominions' and of other colonies
- ▮ Mandates and protectorates of Britain

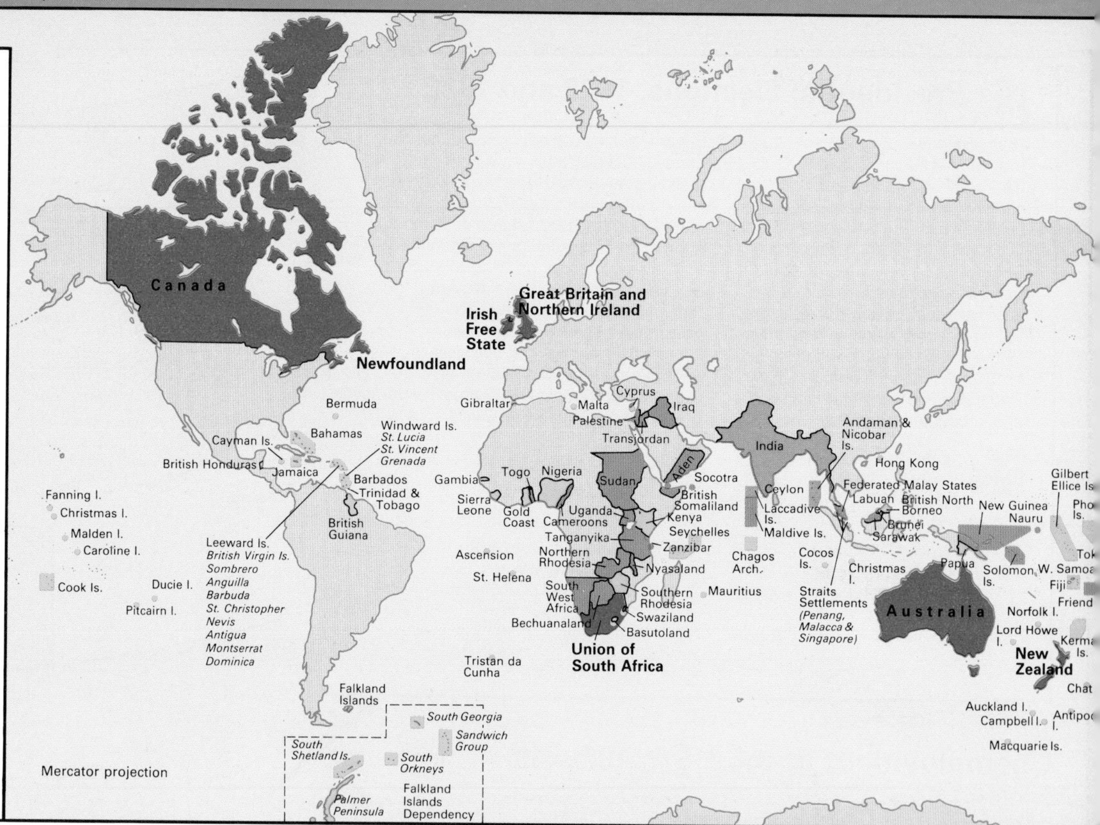

Mercator projection

(World map with labels: Canada, Great Britain and Northern Ireland, Irish Free State, Newfoundland, Bermuda, Gibraltar, Malta, Cyprus, Iraq, Palestine, Transjordan, India, Andaman & Nicobar Is., Hong Kong, Cayman Is., Bahamas, Windward Is. St. Lucia St. Vincent Grenada, British Honduras, Jamaica, Barbados Trinidad & Tobago, Gambia, Togo, Nigeria, Sudan, Aden, Socotra, Ceylon, Federated Malay States, Labuan, British North Borneo, Brunei, Sarawak, New Guinea, Nauru, Gilbert & Ellice Is., British Guiana, Sierra Leone, Gold Coast, Cameroons, Uganda, Kenya, British Somaliland, Laccadive Is., Maldive Is., Fanning I., Christmas I., Malden I., Caroline I., Leeward Is. British Virgin Is. Sombrero Anguilla Barbuda St. Christopher Nevis Antigua Montserrat Dominica, Ascension, Tanganyika, Seychelles, Zanzibar, Northern Rhodesia, Nyasaland, Chagos Arch., Cocos Is., Christmas I., Papua, Solomon Is., W. Samoa, Fiji, Friendly, Cook Is., Ducie I., Pitcairn I., St. Helena, South West Africa, Southern Rhodesia, Mauritius, Straits Settlements (Penang, Malacca & Singapore), Australia, Norfolk I., Lord Howe I., Kermadec Is., Bechuanaland, Swaziland, Basutoland, Union of South Africa, New Zealand, Tristan da Cunha, Falkland Islands, South Georgia, Sandwich Group, South Shetland Is., South Orkneys, Falkland Islands Dependency, Palmer Peninsula, Auckland I., Campbell I., Chatham, Antipodes, Macquarie Is.)

3 Post-war India

One of the earliest of all Afro-Asian nationalist parties was the Indian National Congress. This movement not only provided much of the political impetus to independence; in its modern guise of the Congress Party it has been the main party of government since independence. Relations between Britain and India were embittered by the Amritsar Massacre, when British troops fired on an orderly demonstrating crowd, killing or wounding some 1,500.

The dominant Indian figure from this time was Gandhi. His political philosophy contained two basic messages. One was that the Indians should restore economic self-sufficiency by reviving simple crafts. He adopted the spinning-wheel as a symbol. The second was '*satyagraha*', a belief that truth and justice will ultimately prevail if insisted upon by peaceful pressure. The most famous exposition of this was the great march to collect salt from the sea in protest at the salt-tax.

— Boundary of British India

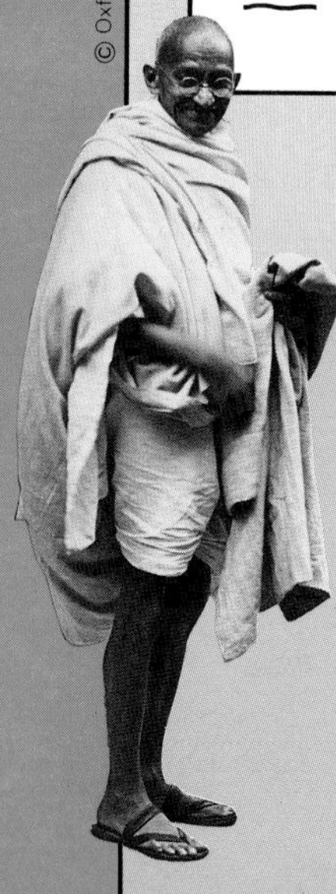

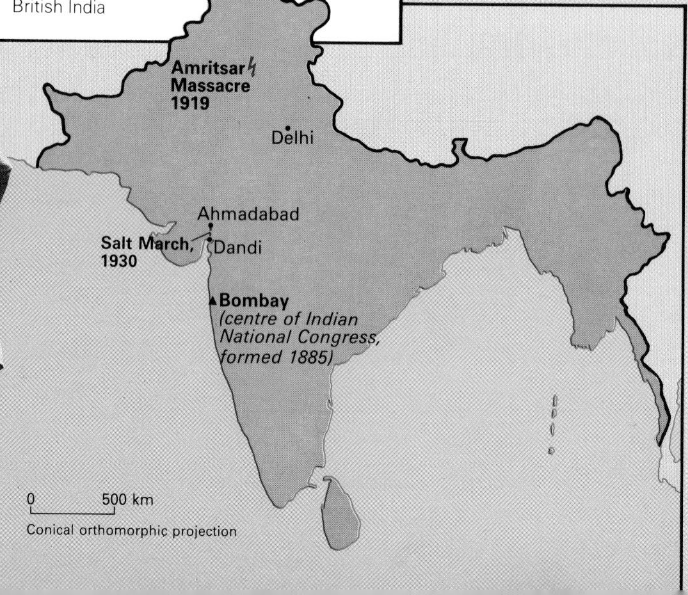

Amritsar Massacre 1919
Delhi
Ahmadabad
Salt March 1930
Dandi
Bombay (centre of Indian National Congress, formed 1885)

0 ___ 500 km
Conical orthomorphic projection

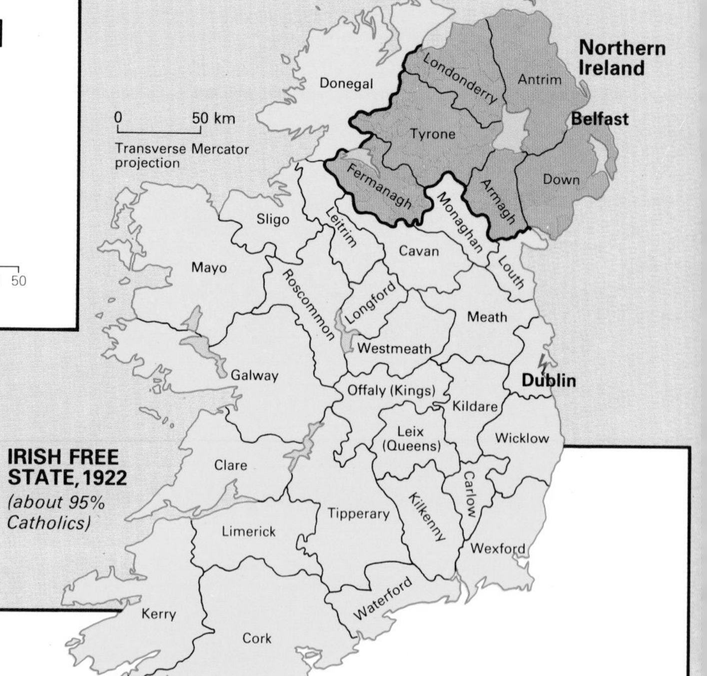

Direction of British trade, 1930

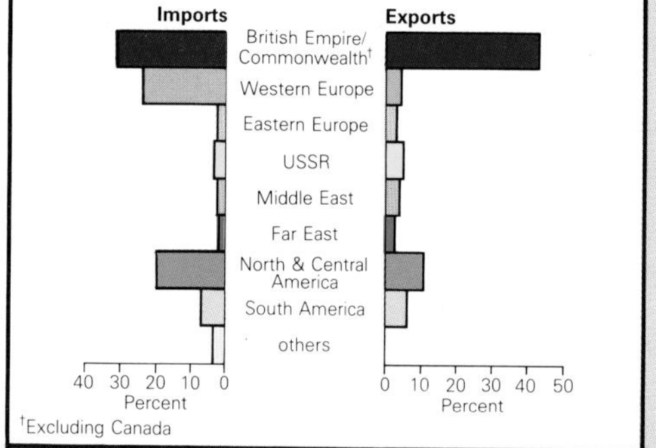

Imports | Exports

- British Empire/Commonwealth[†]
- Western Europe
- Eastern Europe
- USSR
- Middle East
- Far East
- North & Central America
- South America
- others

Imports: 40 30 20 10 0 Percent
Exports: 0 10 20 30 40 50 Percent

†Excluding Canada

(Ireland map with county labels: Donegal, Londonderry, Antrim, Northern Ireland, Belfast, Tyrone, Down, Fermanagh, Armagh, Monaghan, Louth, Sligo, Leitrim, Cavan, Mayo, Roscommon, Longford, Meath, Westmeath, Galway, Offaly (Kings), Kildare, Dublin, Leix (Queens), Wicklow, Clare, Tipperary, Kilkenny, Carlow, Wexford, Limerick, Waterford, Kerry, Cork)

0 ___ 50 km
Transverse Mercator projection

IRISH FREE STATE, 1922 (about 95% Catholics)

2 Post-war Ireland

Nineteenth-century attempts to break British domination over Ireland by the concession of 'Home Rule' nearly came to fruition in 1914, only to be shelved by the onset of the First World War. Frustrated nationalists organized the Easter Week Rebellion in Dublin in 1916 (⚡); the brutality of its suppression further enflamed feelings. The political movement for national independence was called the Sinn Fein; its military wing, was the Irish Republican Army (IRA), which resumed the struggle in 1919.

In 1921 Ireland was partitioned, the mainly Protestant Northern Ireland remaining part of the United Kingdom. The Irish Free state formally came into existence a year later. But the nationalist De Valera rejected the arrangement and encouraged the IRA in this hostility so far as to provoke civil war, 1922–3. However, De Valera became prime minister in 1932 and had himself to cope with IRA violence. In 1937 the country was renamed Eire.

Northern Ireland census, 1911:
- ▮ Catholic regions
- ▮ Protestant regions
- ▬ Partition boundary, 1921
- — County boundaries

4 A Tale of Two Parties

It is sometimes said that there is a naturalness or inevitability in Britain's having a two-party system. Yet political scientists do not agree on whether this is so, or if it is, what the reasons might be. Nevertheless, the failure of the Liberal and Labour Parties to co-exist as alternatives to Conservatives in the inter-war period seemed to confirm the view.

The dramatic decline in electoral support for the Liberals had many reasons. One was the personal quarrel between Asquith and Lloyd George. They were the last two Liberal prime ministers and, between them, were in power for twelve years. Although their quarrel split the party, fundamental divisions in policy were already evident, in any case. Asquith personified the Victorian tradition of government exclusion from economic affairs; Lloyd George, the manipulative role. The confusion was transmitted to the voters.

In the meantime, the Labour Party grew in strength, almost doubling its share of the vote, 1922–35. Crucial to this progress was the adoption of a new, clear Constitution in 1918. As the working class suffered from the industrial disputes of the 1920s and the unemployment of the 1930s the Labour Party came increasingly to seem the natural left-wing movement to cater for their needs. Not that the Labour Party was any more homogeneous in its political doctrines than the Liberals. Indeed, its unity was sorely strained by the experience of office. Ramsay Macdonald became prime minister of Labour governments in 1924 and 1929–31. In 1929, Labour had 287 MPs compared with the Liberals' 59. However, the appalling economic problems of the time forced him to seek Conservative allies and in 1931–5 he headed a National government. Staunch Socialists in the Labour movement branded him a traitor to their cause.

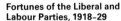

Decline of the Liberals, 1922–45

Fortunes of the Liberal and Labour Parties, 1918–29

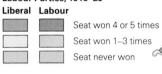

Liberal	Labour	
		Seat won 4 or 5 times
		Seat won 1–3 times
		Seat never won

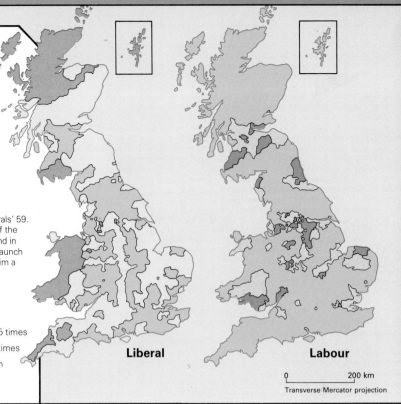

Liberal   Labour

0   200 km

Transverse Mercator projection

Unemployment and government spending

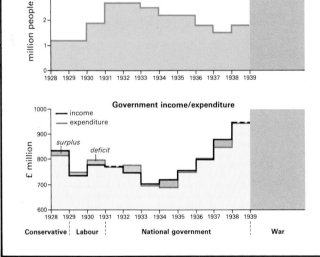

Number unemployed

Government income/expenditure

Conservative | Labour | National government | War

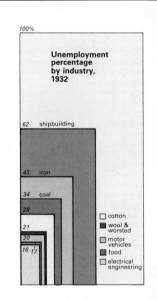

Unemployment percentage by industry, 1932

62 shipbuilding
43 iron
34 coal
28
21
20
16 17

□ cotton
■ wool & worsted
□ motor vehicles
□ food
□ electrical engineering

Unemployment (by county)

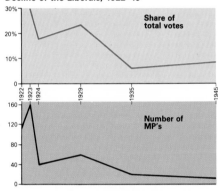

- 45% and over
- 35–45%
- 25–35%
- 15–25%
- less than 15%
- Routes of National Hunger March, October 1937
- Route of Jarrow March, 1936

Glasgow
Newcastle
Jarrow
Middlesbrough
Burnley
Liverpool
Manchester
Sheffield
Mansfield
Stoke-on-Trent
Birmingham
Norwich
Hereford
Cardif
Bristol
London
Canterbury
Southampton
Brighton
Plymouth

0   200 km
Transverse Mercator projection

5 The Post-war British Economy

The strength of Britain's industry and international trade was already beginning to wane by the turn of the century in the face of competition from the USA and Germany. Where Britain's share of world trade had been 33 per cent in 1870, it had shrunk to 14 per cent by 1914. After the First World War the trend was aggravated by a number of factors. Concentration on the war effort itself enabled competitors to infiltrate former British markets. British goods were also overpriced. Then, after the Wall Street Crash of 1929, world-wide depression contracted demand for the kinds of goods Britain had for sale. Compared with a respectable average annual trade balance of more than £60 million in the 1920s, the UK plunged into an average deficit of £100 million per year in the 1930s.

As the flow of orders dried up, so firms laid off their men or even went out of business completely. Unemployment, which stood at 1.2 million in 1928, rose to 2.7 million by 1932. However, broad figures mask the huge regional variations and thus the misery wrought in those areas most affected. Only 1 in 20 were unemployed in Coventry in 1934 compared with two-thirds in the stricken ship-building town of Jarrow. The 'Jarrow March' was the most famous of the great demonstrations of the unemployed in the 1930s demanding some form of government action.

The crisis gradually eased. One of the crucial factors in the reduction of unemployment was a great building boom, as slums were torn down, and houses and public buildings like cinemas were constructed.

Dublin
GREAT BRITAIN
IRISH FREE STATE (EIRE, 1937)
London
NETHERLANDS
BELGIUM
Paris
LUXEMBOURG
FRANCE
SWITZERLAND
PORTUGAL 1926
Lisbon
Madrid
SPAIN (1923–30) 1938
NORWAY
Oslo
SWEDEN
Stockholm
FINLAND
Helsinki
DENMARK
Copenhagen
ESTONIA 1934
LATVIA 1934
(1926–9) LITHUANIA 1936
Berlin
Danzig
Warsaw
1933
Weimar
POLAND 1926
Prague
CZECHOSLOVAKIA
Vienna
AUSTRIA 1933
Budapest
HUMGARY
ROMANIA 1938
Bucharest
YUGOSLAVIA 1929
Belgrade
BULGARIA (1923–30)
Sofia
ITALY
Rome 1922
ALBANIA 1925
GREECE 1936
Athens
TURKEY 1922
U.S.S.R.

0   500 km
Conical orthomorphic projection

1 The Decline of Democracy in Europe, 1919–38

After the entry of the USA into and the withdrawal of Russia from the First World War many people felt that the conflict was between the authoritarian Central Powers and the democratic Allies. And when, after the war, the states of central and eastern Europe drew up new constitutions, most were indeed democratic in style. Yet many of these proved to be quite short-lived. Democracy requires a tolerant political give-and-take. But fear of electoral defeat sometimes means hesitation to take decisive action. Europe suffered serious difficulties in the 1920s: several states were new; and economic troubles rocked even quite stable governments, especially after the crisis of 1929. And citizens who had not been used to democracy became impatient at the failure of their politicians to cope.
Political parties like the Fascists in Italy and Nazis in Germany, who promised strong government, seemed to many people more attractive. At the same time new political ideas and techniques were being developed. Political police instilled fear in opponents; and propaganda mobilized the

support of the waverers. Theories of racial distinctiveness and the infallibility of the leader, for example, justified these regimes, which have sometimes been called totalitarian because the whole of life was controlled. Often, however, the authoritarian governments were not as efficient as they liked to claim. One reason for this was that political power was concentrated in the hands of dictators. These included Mussolini in Italy, Hitler in Germany, Stalin in the USSR, Pilsudski in Poland, Salazar in Portugal, Franco in Spain. It is difficult, however, for one man always to make wise decisions. Even so, barely a dozen European states could be called democratic in 1939 (and then only if one counts Hungary, whose democratic system was very frail throughout the whole period).

Democracy suppressed between 1919 and 1938

Temporary dictatorship before 1930

■ Capital city

International boundary from 1923

3 Germany begins to stir, 1920–36

R. Elbe
R. Oder
R. Rhine
GERMANY
Nuremberg (Nazi rallies here from 1927)
Munich (1923 Putsch)

0   200 km
Conical orthomorphic projection

General conscription introduced 16 March 1935

The defeat of Germany in the First World War left a legacy of resentment, both against the politicians who agreed to the Versailles Settlement and the foreign states who imposed it (Unit 9). 1923 was a year of crisis for the German government. Because the country was behind with its payments of reparations the French occupied the industrial area of the Ruhr. Also attempts were made in some parts of Germany to set up governments independent of Weimar (the seat of the German National Assembly). The most serious was the Nazi putsch (attempted seizure of power) in Munich. The demonstrators were dispersed and their leader, Hitler, was imprisoned.

While in prison Hitler started to write Mein Kampf (My Struggle). He described his beliefs and plans. These included the idea that the Germans were the Aryan Master Race and that their destiny to lead the world was threatened by Jews and Communists. He denounced the Versailles Settlement and promised to make Germany great again.
Hitler was soon released and worked energetically to build up the strength of the Nazi party. This was partly achieved by painstaking organization of party administration throughout the country; partly by vigorous recruitment and rallies of members; and partly by intimidation of opponents by the brown-shirted 'Stormtroopers'. Mounting unemployment from 1929 to 1933, caused by the economic depression, made an increasing number of Germans turn to the Nazis in the hope of improvement. The number of Nazi deputies in the Reichstag (parliament) rose from 12 in 1928 to 233 in 1933. Because the Nazis were the largest party in the Reichstag, Hitler was made Chancellor (prime minister) in 1933. The next month the Reichstag building was set on fire. The Nazis blamed the Communist Party and declared it illegal. Hitler quickly assumed many powers personally as Führer and eliminated his rivals within the party in the 'Night of the Long Knives' in 1934.
The Nazi government soon reduced unemployment by building up the armed forces (contrary to the Versailles Treaty) and by public works like road-building. In foreign policy Hitler defied Britain and France as guarantors of the Versailles Settlement by sending troops into the Rhineland, an area specifically demilitarized by that treaty.

Boundary of Germany, 1914

International boundaries after Versailles, 1920

Territory lost by Germany, 1919

Plebiscite areas

Areas under armed occupation

Areas under League of Nations High Commissioners

Areas where Nazis gained a majority in elections, November 1932

卐 Places of initial Nazi support in Bavaria

Germans unemployed, 1933–7

	millions
October 1933	6.0
October 1934	4.1
February 1935	2.8
February 1936	2.5
February 1937	1.2

The Nazis gathered much support from the middle class by emphasizing the threat from Communism. This cover of a magazine, published in January 1933, suggests that Russian schoolchildren are being given military training in readiness to attack an unprepared Germany.

Illustrierter Beobachter
VERLAG FRZ. EHER NACHF. 27. MÜNCHEN 2 NO
Russland rüstet! ...und Deutschland?

2 The Search for Security, 1920–36

The bloodshed of the First World War was a great shock. And despite the League of Nations (or because of its weakness), the states of Europe desperately tried to ensure their own security by treaties in the event of renewed international tension. These either aimed to resolve quarrels or to pledge mutual military support. Within the complicated tangles of these treaties two constant concerns may be noted. One is the French worry about protecting themselves against a possible German military revival (e.g. Locarno). The other is the fear of a number of east European states that, because of their ethnic minorities, attempts might be made to change their boundaries (e.g. Little Entente, Balkan Pact).

⟋⟍	International boundaries
⟁—⟁	French alliances
⟁—⟁	German alliances
⟁—⟁	Italian alliances
⟁—⟁	Soviet alliances
⟁—⟁	Little Entente, 1920/1
⟁—⟁	Baltic Entente, 1922
⟁—⟁	Locarno Treaties, 1925
⟁—⟁	Balkan Pact, 1934
⟁—⟁	Stresa Front, 1935
⟁—⟁	Naval Agreement 1935

European treaties and alliances, 1920–35

1920 Franco–Belgian; Czech–Yugoslav (both anti-Germany, pro E. Europe).
1921 *Little Entente*: Czechoslovakia–Romania/ Romania–Yugoslavia (anti-Hungary); Franco–Polish/ Polish–Romanian (anti-Hungary).
1922 *Baltic Entente*: Poland–Estonia–Latvia–Finland (anti-USSR); *Rapallo Treaty*: Germany–USSR (*see also* Treaty of Berlin).
1924 *Adriatic Treaty*: Italy–Yugoslavia (Mussolini's '*status quo*'); Franco–Czech.
1925 *Locarno Treaties*: Germany–Belgium/Germany– France/Germany–Poland/Germany–Czechoslovakia (guaranteed Western boundary of Germany); Franco– Polish; Franco–Czech.
1926 Franco–Romanian; *Treaty of Berlin*: Germany– USSR; *Italy–Albania Pact*; *Treaty of Friendship*: Italy–Romania (recognition of Bessarabia).

1927 Italian–Albanian (Albanian 'independence'); Italian–Hungarian (anti-Yugoslavia); Franco–Yugoslav.
1928 Italian–Turkish; Italian–Greek.
1930 *Treaty of Friendship*: Italy–Austria.
1932 *Treaty of Arbitration and Non-aggression Pact*: France–USSR; Soviet–Finnish; Soviet– Estonian; Soviet– Latvian; Soviet–Polish.
1934 *Balkan Pact*: Yugoslavia–Romania–Turkey– Greece (anti Nazi/Bulgar/USSR); *Rome Protocols* Italy–Austria/Italy–Hungary (Italy flexing its muscles); German–Polish Non-aggression Treaty (upset French alliance system).
1935 Franco-Russian Mutual Assistance Treaty (anti-Germany); *Stresa Front*: Great Britain–France–Italy; *Naval Agreement*: Great Britain-Germany.

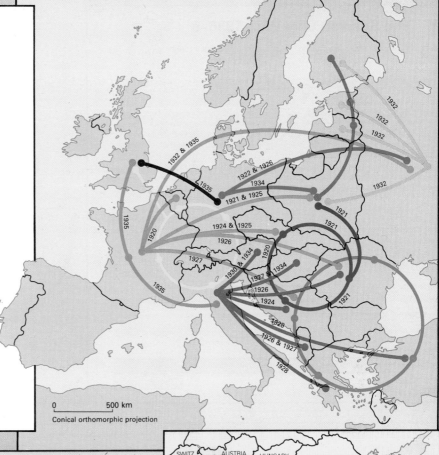

Conical orthomorphic projection

5 The Italian Invasion of Abyssinia, 1935–6

Mussolini extended the Italian empire a little in the Mediterranean (*map 4*). But the most controversial part of his imperial policy was the use of modern weapons, including poison gas, against the primitively-armed Abyssinians. In December 1934 the Italians arranged a 'frontier incident' at Wal Wal and invaded in October 1935. The British and French tried ineffectually to bring about peace: by proposing economic sanctions and by the Hoare-Laval plan for partition.

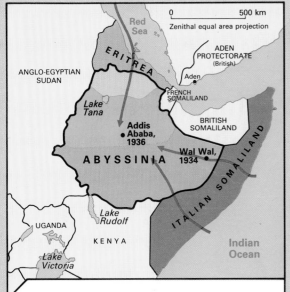

⟋⟍	Abyssinia, 1934	
→	Italian advances	
⟋⟍	Other international boundaries, 1934	

Hoare-Laval Plan, 1935:

- Reduced size of Abyssinia
- Area to be given to Eritrea
- Area to be given to Italian Somaliland

4 The Rise of Italian Fascism, 1919–36

- Territory acquired by Italy to 1939
- ⟋⟍ International boundaries, 1923

Conical orthomorphic projection

Mussolini founded the Fascist Party in 1919 and, after violent demonstrations, including 'the March on Rome', took control of the government in 1922. He was thus one of the earliest of the twentieth-century European dictators. He took the title, *Il Duce'* (the Leader), and promised to restore the glories of the Roman Empire. Italy became a 'corporative state', that is, people were required to join trade unions and professional organizations, which were controlled by the government. There was no political freedom. Opponents were treated brutally and newspapers were censored. Mussolini did try to improve the economy, for example, by making the Pontine Marshes fertile and generally improving grain production. He also signed the Lateran Treaties, by which the Pope agreed that his only territory was Vatican City.

- ▢ Main areas of growth of the Fascist Party in Italy, 1919–21
- • Fascist squads in action before October 1922
- + Fascist takeover of provincial administration, October 1922
- → March on Rome, 1922

1 The Spanish Civil War, 1936-9

There was a great deal of quarrelling and discontent in Spain in the 1930s; and when a left-wing government came to power in 1936, the Falangists (Fascist party), the Church, the wealthy and many army officers bitterly disapproved. General Franco, who commanded the army in Spanish Morocco, returned with a view to overthrowing the government. The result was a civil war between right-wing Nationalist forces and left-wing Republican.

The official policy of the main European governments was non-intervention—to prevent the war from expanding into a general European conflict. In pursuit of this policy naval squadrons patrolled Spanish waters to prevent the supply of weapons. However, the war aroused strong feelings throughout Europe. Many who sympathized with the government, for example the English novelist George Orwell, fought as volunteers on the Republican side (the International Brigade). Various European governments also in fact had decided preferences. The Soviet Union helped the government. But Italian and particularly German 'volunteers' to the Nationalists were more effective. Especially important was the provision of air support by the German Condor Legion. This led to the most notorious event of the war, namely the bombing of Guernica (⚡), a defenceless Basque town.

The war was strenuously contested on both sides and much damage and many casualties were caused. Probably well over half a million people died. But eventually the Nationalists won. Franco became dictator and remained in control of the government until his death in 1975.

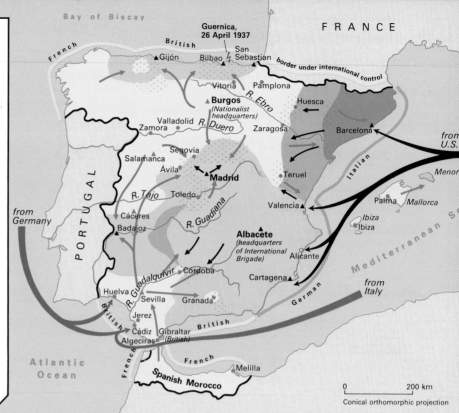

Guernica, 26 April 1937

| Boundary of Spain, 1936 | | | |

Nationalist: ▲ bases   ➡ supply routes   → attacks
Republican: ▲ bases   ➡ supply routes   → attacks
Naval patrols: British/French   Italian/German

Areas of intensive fighting   • Successful Nationalist risings, July 1936

Areas of control

Nationalists	by July 1936	by Oct. 1937	by July 1938	by Feb. 1939
Republicans				by Feb. 1939

0 —— 200 km
Conical orthomorphic projection

2 The Ambitions of Germany, 1936

Although the basic principle of the Paris peace treaties (*Unit 9*) was national self-determination, the Germans were not allowed its complete implementation. Union (*Anschluss*) with Austria was expressly forbidden and many German-speaking people found themselves as minorities in neighbouring states. Hitler was able to rouse considerable sympathy both in Germany and abroad for his claim that such people had a right to join their fatherland. He was particularly keen to bring about the *Anschluss*, partly because it related to his campaign against the Versailles Settlement and partly because he was himself born just inside the Austrian border.

The map shown here is taken from an atlas published in Berlin in 1936. It shows the areas which were considered by the Nazi government as rightfully German—either by the test of language or by the vaguer definition of culture.

| Boundary of Germany, 1936 | Other international boundaries, 1936 |

'German Culture territory'
'German Speaking territory' } from a Berlin atlas of 1936

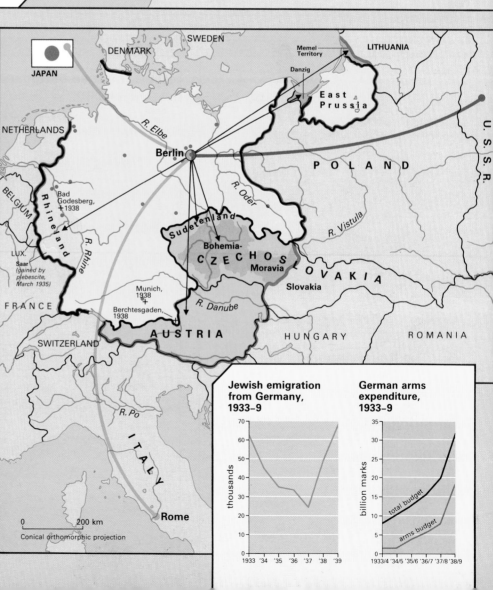

Jewish emigration from Germany, 1933-9

(thousands)
70
60
50
40
30
20
10
0
1933 '34 '35 '36 '37 '38 '39

German arms expenditure, 1933-9

(billion marks)
35
30
25
20
15
10
5
0
1933/4 '34/5 '35/6 '36/7 '37/8 '38/9

total budget
arms budget

0 —— 200 km
Conical orthomorphic projection

4 The Killing of Two Countries, 1938–9

Poland

— Boundary of Poland, 1937

⌇ Other international boundaries, 1937

▦ Area seized from Czechoslovakia, October 1938

▨ Annexed by Germany / Seized by USSR ⎫ September 1939

— Russo-German Pact line

▨ The rest of Poland—a German dependency by October 1939

▪▪▪▪ Curzon line of 1919

Czechoslovakia

— Boundary of Czechoslovakia, 1937

⌇ Other international boundaries, 1937

▨ Surrendered to Germany, October 1938 / Seized by Poland, October 1938

▨ Seized by Hungary, November 1938 / Seized by Hungary, March/April 1939

▨ The German protectorates of Bohemia-Moravia (with the *Reich*) and Slovakia (nominally independent), March 1939

3 Germany's Challenge, 1936–9

The tempo of Nazi violence accelerated, 1936–9. The persecution of the Jews intensified especially after 'Kristallnacht' (the smashing of windows) in 1938. Hence the increase in emigration.
In foreign affairs Hitler pursued a policy of friendship with Italy and Japan, a grouping which came to be called the Axis. He also took opportunities to pursue a German nationalist policy: March 1936—remilitarization of the Rhineland (Unit 9); March 1938—Anschluss with Austria; October 1938—occupation of the Sudetenland; March 1939—occupation of Bohemia-Moravia, Danzig and Memel; September 1939—invasion of Poland.
These events led to the start of the Second World War, triggered by the invasion of Poland. Britain and France have been criticized for failing to stop Hitler when he was militarily weak but reoccupied the Rhineland. And the British prime minister, Chamberlain, has been criticized for his policy of 'appeasement'. He flew to Berchtesgaden, Bad Godesberg and Munich for talks with Hitler, but in vain. However, the question also arises whether Hitler was deliberately planning war. The fact that his armaments budget was not substantially increased until 1938 suggests that he might have had a date later than 1939 in mind.

Boundary of Germany:
— 1936 ━ 1939

German expansion:
→1936 →1938 →1939

●━● Anti-Comintern Pact
●━● Non-Aggression Pact
● Concentration camps built 1933–7

5 The Search for Security Continues, 1936–9

As the acts of aggression by Germany, Italy (Unit 14) and Japan (Unit 11) multiplied these three countries grew closer together. Britain and France started to prepare for war, but failed to make common cause with the Soviet Union, whose policies under Stalin they found objectionable. The Soviets instead made a treaty with Germany, one of the terms of which arranged for the partition of Poland (Map 4).

▨ 'Berlin-Rome Axis' powers
●━● Anti-Comintern Pact
●━● 'Pact of Steel'
●━● Non-Aggression Pact
▨ Britain and France
●━● Anglo-Egyptian Treaty
▨ Countries guaranteed by Britain and France, 1939
●━● Anglo-French alliances
+ Anglo-French staff talks, April 1936–June 1939

Declarations of neutrality
▨ Belgium (1936) joined by other countries, July 1938
⌇ International boundaries, 1936

The struggle to catch up

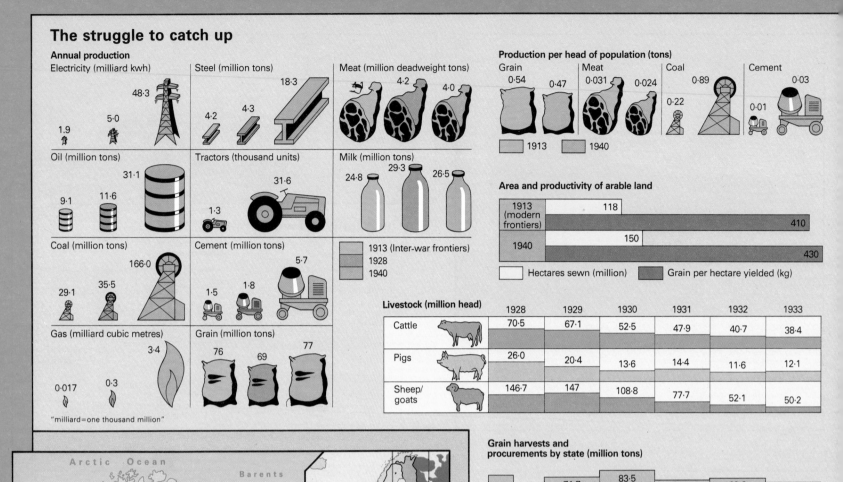

Annual production

Electricity (milliard kwh): 1.9, 5.0, 48.3

Steel (million tons): 4.2, 4.3, 18.3

Meat (million deadweight tons): 4.2, 4.0

Oil (million tons): 9.1, 11.6, 31.1

Tractors (thousand units): 1.3, 31.6

Milk (million tons): 24.8, 29.3, 26.5

Coal (million tons): 29.1, 35.5, 166.0

Cement (million tons): 1.5, 1.8, 5.7

Gas (milliard cubic metres): 0.017, 0.3, 3.4

Grain (million tons): 76, 69, 77

Legend:
- 1913 (Inter-war frontiers)
- 1928
- 1940

"milliard = one thousand million"

Production per head of population (tons)

	Grain	Meat	Coal	Cement
1913	0.54	0.031	0.22	0.01
1940	0.47	0.024	0.89	0.03

Area and productivity of arable land

	Hectares sewn (million)	Grain per hectare yielded (kg)
1913 (modern frontiers)	118	410
1940	150	430

Livestock (million head)

	1928	1929	1930	1931	1932	1933
Cattle	70.5	67.1	52.5	47.9	40.7	38.4
Pigs	26.0	20.4	13.6	14.4	11.6	12.1
Sheep/goats	146.7	147	108.8	77.7	52.1	50.2

Grain harvests and procurements by state (million tons)

	1929	1930	1931	1932	1933
Harvest	71.7	83.5	69.5	69.6	68.4
Procurement	16.1	22.1	22.8	18.5	22.6

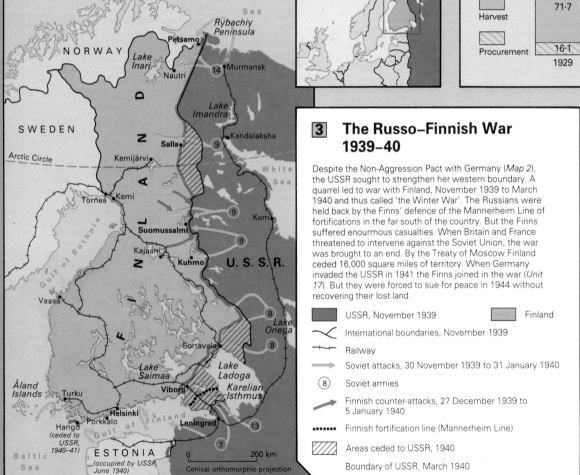

3 The Russo–Finnish War 1939–40

Despite the Non-Aggression Pact with Germany (*Map 2*), the USSR sought to strengthen her western boundary. A quarrel led to war with Finland, November 1939 to March 1940 and thus called 'the Winter War'. The Russians were held back by the Finns' defence of the Mannerheim Line of fortifications in the far south of the country. But the Finns suffered enourmous casualties. When Britain and France threatened to intervene against the Soviet Union, the war was brought to an end. By the Treaty of Moscow Finland ceded 16,000 square miles of territory. When Germany invaded the USSR in 1941 the Finns joined in the war (*Unit 17*). But they were forced to sue for peace in 1944 without recovering their lost land.

Legend:
- USSR, November 1939
- Finland
- International boundaries, November 1939
- Railway
- Soviet attacks, 30 November 1939 to 31 January 1940
- 8 Soviet armies
- Finnish counter-attacks, 27 December 1939 to 5 January 1940
- Finnish fortification line (Mannerheim Line)
- Areas ceded to USSR, 1940
- Boundary of USSR, March 1940

The Marxist theory of Communism foretells the collapse of the capitalist economic system. Stalin feared that capitalist states like the USA, Britain and France would try to stave off this crisis by attacking the Soviet Union. The most hostile criticisms of the Soviet Union were expressed by Hitler. Therefore, as he was coming to power, some German industrialists and the capitalists of other Western countries tended to support him. This Soviet cartoon of 1936 shows the capitalist 'fairy-godfathers' looking benignly upon the politically-infant Hitler, despite the jackboot and dagger—evidence of his brutal methods.

1 The Russian Search for Security

The figures in 'A struggle to catch up' reveal a massive concentration of effort on heavy industry. Stalin believed that the hatred and fear of Communism felt by the capitalist governments in the West would lead them to attack the Soviet Union. A strong industry was necessary for building up the armed forces. He also used diplomatic means for protection. The Treaty of Moscow brought seven states of eastern Europe and the Middle East into alliance with the USSR.

However, by the early 1930s, fearful particularly of the rise of a militaristic and expansionist Japan (*Unit 11*), Stalin became prepared for friendlier relations with the Western democracies. This change of policy suited Litvinov, Commissar for Foreign Affairs, 1930–39: in

1920 he had coined the phrase, 'Peace is indivisible'. From 1932 to 1935 the policy materialized in a number of diplomatic successes. The collection of non-aggression pacts signed in 1932 included France as well as the USSR's immediate western neighbours. In 1932 the USA, who had shunned the Bolshevik government, now formally recognized the USSR; they shared the fear of Japan. In 1934 the USSR became a member of the League of Nations, a body largely influenced by Britain and France. In 1935 Soviet friendship with France was cemented by a new pact. This was made easier by Stalin's change of policy towards other Communist Parties. He encouraged some, like the French, to co-operate with 'bourgeois' parties to form 'Popular Front' governments.

- ▨ USSR, 1929
- ▧ Signatories to the Moscow Treaty, 1929
- ⚊●⚊ Non-Aggression treaties, 1932
- ⚊●⚊ Mutual Assistance Treaty, 1935
- ⌒ International boundaries, 1929

1933 USA recognizes USSR
1934 USSR joins the League of Nations

boundary 'guaranteed' since 1920

0 ___ 500 km

Conical orthomorphic projection

Hitler's Nazism and Stalin's Communism were mutually antagonistic ideologies. Nevertheless, for their own convenience they signed a pact in August 1939 (*see Map 2*) and used it to dismember Poland. This famous cartoon by the English artist, David Low, shows the two leaders as hypocritical friends greeting each other over the body of Poland.

2 The Russian Land-grab, 1939–40

In August 1939 the German Foreign Minister, von Ribbentrop, met the new Soviet Foreign Minister, V. M. Molotov in Moscow. They signed a non-aggression pact. Each side agreed to remain neutral if the other was involved in a war. More important, however, were the secret clauses, slightly amended the following month. These allowed for the partition of Poland between the two signatories and for the Soviet Union to extend its influence into the Baltic states, Finland and the Bessarabian province of Romania. The Treaty was of major significance. Stalin, shocked by the Western policy of appeasement towards Hitler at Munich (*see unit 15*), was now resigned to a war between Germany and the Western democracies. He took the opportunity at least to postpone Soviet involvement in a conflict with Nazi Germany, which Hitler's policy seemed likely to bring about (*see Unit 17*). Hitler, meanwhile, saw the agreement as a means of gaining Poland without risking war with the USSR. By thus securing his eastern flank Hitler had confidence to invade Poland on 1st September 1939, an action which triggered the outbreak of the Second World War (*Unit 17*).

From September 1939 to July 1940 the Soviet Union absorbed a large amount of land, thus pushing her frontier a considerable distance to the west and rendering the major cities of Moscow and Leningrad rather less vulnerable in the event of an invasion. After the German attack on Poland in the west, the USSR invaded from the

east. Polish resistance was overcome by 3rd October. The following month the USSR attacked Finland (*see Map 3*). The annexations of the Baltic states of Estonia, Latvia and Lithuania and of Northern Bukovina and Bessarabia from Romania in the summer of 1940 completed this policy of expansion.

Stalin has often been criticized for these seizures of territory and Baltic nationalists are still demanding autonomy for their peoples. On the other hand, the extra land helped when the German invasion occurred in 1941. Also, it must be remembered, the whole of Finland, the Baltic states and the lands taken from Poland and Romania had been parts of the nineteenth-century Russian empire (*see Unit 2*).

- ⌒ International boundaries, August 1939
- ▨ USSR, August 1939
- ⚊●⚊ German–Soviet Non-Aggression Pact, 23 August 1939

Land occupied by USSR

September 1939	March 1940	June 1940	July 1940
(occupied)	(ceded)	(ceded)	(annexed)

- ⚍ Boundary of USSR, August 1940

1 Europe under Blitzkrieg, 1939–41

'Blitzkrieg' means 'lightning war'. The Germans mastered a technique of rapid advance with tanks, motorized infantry and close air support. Poland was overwhelmed in this way. But from October 1939 to April 1940 there was little action: the period of the 'phoney war'. Then, in very rapid succession, the Germans captured Denmark, Norway and the Low Countries in blitzkrieg campaigns. The failure of the British effectively to support Norway led to the replacement of Neville Chamberlain as prime minister by Winston Churchill. France resisted a little more successfully but collapsed after six weeks. British troops sent to assist were encircled at Dunkirk, but were rescued by a fleet of small vessels crossing the Channel. France was partitioned. A government friendly to the Germans was established under Marshal Pétain at Vichy.
Italy entered the war in June 1940. But her unsuccessful invasion of Greece and Egypt led to German intervention. By June 1941

Germany controlled the Balkans through allies or occupation; and her Afrika Korps had reversed the British advance in Libya.

- ⌒ International boundaries, September 1939
- ▢ Germany and Italy (Axis Powers), 1 September 1939
- ▨ Axis satellites and allies Axis-occupied territories, 1939–41
- ▨ USSR, September 1939 USSR-occupied territories, 1939–40
- ▢ British Empire
- ▨ Vichy France created, June 1940
- ▨ Neutral powers
- ⊣⊢ Iron ore railway

Advances:	German		Italian		Allies		Soviet	
1939	➡	September					⇨	September
1940	➡	April–June	▸▸▸	June	➤	April	⇨	June
			••▸	Oct.				
1941	➡	February–April			➤	Feb.		
	➡	April–May						

↩ Allied retreat May 1940

3 The Holocaust

By 1941 the Nazis were in control of so much of Europe that they were able to take their anti-Semitic campaign (see Unit 15) to 'the Final Solution'. This was the systematic annihilation of all Jews, an experience they have called the Holocaust. The task was entrusted to units of the SS under the command of Heydrich. They organized concentration and extermination camps, mainly in eastern Europe. Here the Jews were treated brutally then murdered, many in gas chambers. With the invasion of the USSR special Einsatzgruppen followed the armies to exterminate the Jews there. Altogether nearly six million perished.

- ⌒ International boundaries, December 1939
- ⋯ Boundaries of Ukraine and White Russia, 1939

Hitler's 'New Order' in Europe

- ▢ Greater Germany by November 1942
- ▢ Annexed territories
- ▢ Protectorates
- ⌒ Other international boundaries by 1942
- ▨ Areas under German rule
- ▨ Areas under military occupation by Axis powers
- ▨ Axis allies and satellites

The 'Final Solution'

- ▨ Area where ghettos and work-camps were established for Jews
- ▲ Main concentration and/or extermination camps
- ➡ Advance of the Einsatzgruppen (Action Groups) behind the German armies
- ▢ Countries which successfully resisted the 'Final Solution'
- **450** Numbers of Jews exterminated (in thousands) shown by 1939 political units

B-M = Bohemia-Moravia

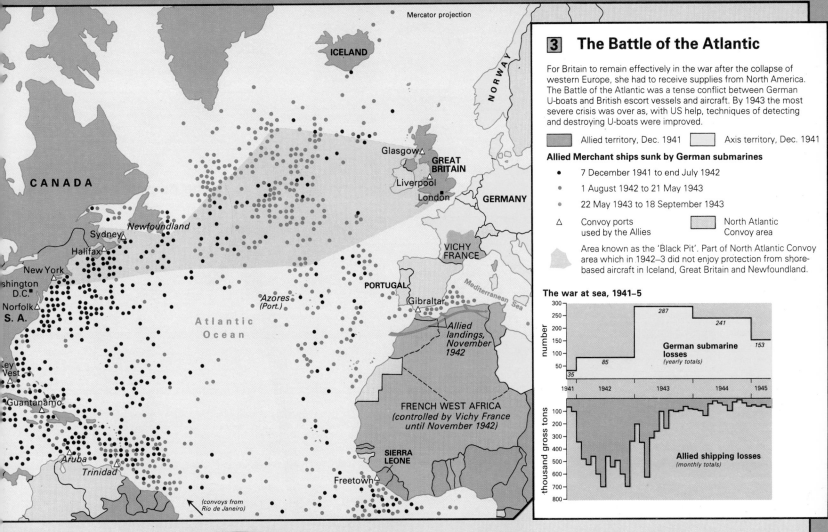

3   The Battle of the Atlantic

For Britain to remain effectively in the war after the collapse of western Europe, she had to receive supplies from North America. The Battle of the Atlantic was a tense conflict between German U-boats and British escort vessels and aircraft. By 1943 the most severe crisis was over as, with US help, techniques of detecting and destroying U-boats were improved.

▨ Allied territory, Dec. 1941   ▢ Axis territory, Dec. 1941

Allied Merchant ships sunk by German submarines

- •   7 December 1941 to end July 1942
- •   1 August 1942 to 21 May 1943
- •   22 May 1943 to 18 September 1943

△   Convoy ports used by the Allies   ▨ North Atlantic Convoy area

Area known as the 'Black Pit'. Part of North Atlantic Convoy area which in 1942–3 did not enjoy protection from shore-based aircraft in Iceland, Great Britain and Newfoundland.

The war at sea, 1941–5

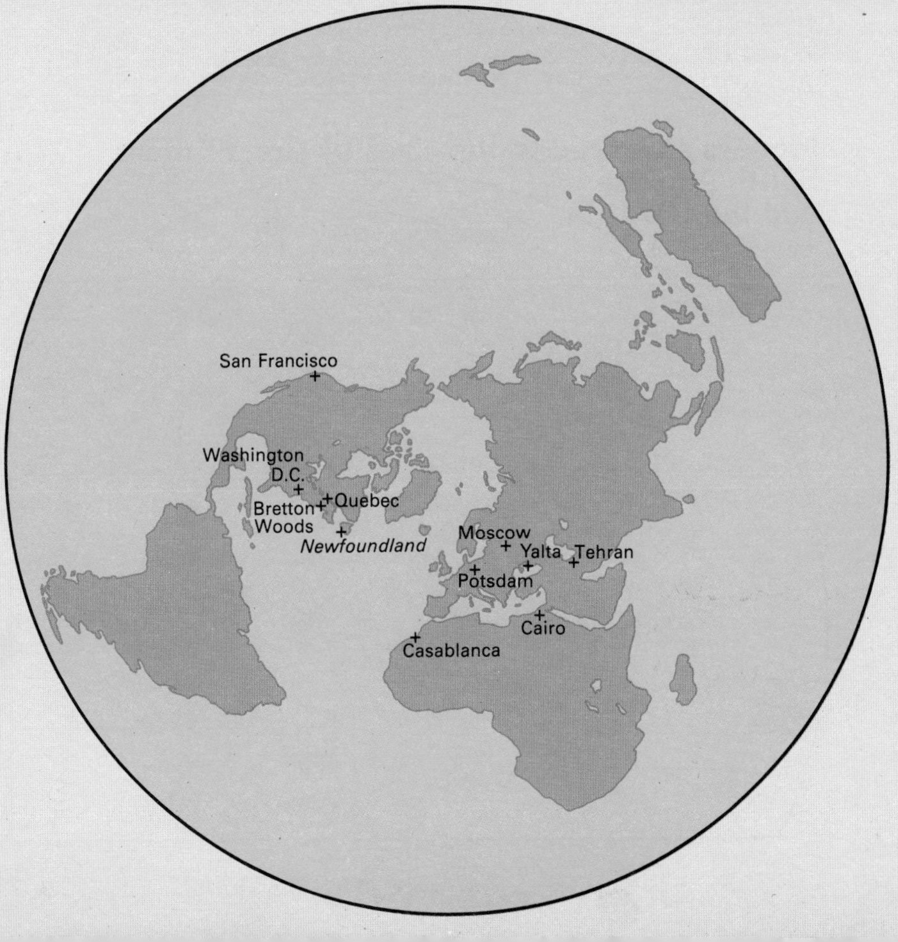

German submarine losses (yearly totals): 35 (1941); 85, 287 (1942–3 area); 241; 153 (1945)

Allied shipping losses (monthly totals) — thousand gross tons

Map labels: Mercator projection; ICELAND; NORWAY; CANADA; Newfoundland; Sydney; Halifax; New York; Washington D.C.; Norfolk; S.A.; ...ey West; Guantanamo; Aruba; Trinidad; (convoys from Rio de Janeiro); Azores (Port.); Atlantic Ocean; Glasgow; GREAT BRITAIN; Liverpool; London; GERMANY; VICHY FRANCE; PORTUGAL; Gibraltar; Mediterranean Sea; Allied landings, November 1942; FRENCH WEST AFRICA (controlled by Vichy France until November 1942); SIERRA LEONE; Freetown

4   Allied Conferences, 1941–5

The Allied leaders were faced with difficult decisions concerning both strategic priorities to be pursued in the conduct of the war and arrangements to be made to render the post-war world more just and harmonious. As the table shows Churchill and Roosevelt met on several occasions. They became personally very friendly, despite Roosevelt's dislike of British imperialism and Churchill's attachment to the Commonwealth. Relations between Churchill and Stalin were less cordial. The cause was partly ideological (they represented the opposed capitalist and Communist systems) and partly suspicion of each other's practical motives. Stalin was bitter that Churchill seemed to delay opening a 'second front' in western Europe to relieve pressure on the embattled Red Army. Churchill in turn suspected Stalin of wishing to control Poland and other parts of eastern Europe. The Yalta Conference was the most controversial: some politicians and historians, rather unfairly, have believed that Stalin outmanoeuvred his Western allies and thus came to create satellite Communist governments throughout eastern Europe.

Globe map labels: San Francisco; Washington D.C.; Bretton Woods; Quebec; Newfoundland; Moscow; Yalta; Tehran; Potsdam; Cairo; Casablanca

Place	Date	Main Participants	Main Agenda Items
Newfoundland	August 1941	Churchill, Roosevelt	General survey of war situation and drafting of the Atlantic Charter to define their war aims.
Washington	December 1941	Churchill, Roosevelt	Establishment of Combined Chiefs of Staff and decision to give priority to war in Europe.
Casablanca	January 1943	Churchill, Roosevelt	General war strategy and agreement on demand for 'unconditional surrender' of the Axis.
Cairo	November 1943	Churchill, Chiang Kai-shek, Roosevelt	The war against Japan.
Tehran	November/December 1943	Churchill, Roosevelt, Stalin	Invasion of western Europe; possible Soviet entry into war against Japan; post-war international organization.
Bretton Woods	July 1944	Representatives of 28 states	Arrangements for the establishment of the International Monetary Fund and World Bank
Quebec	1. August 1943 2. September 1944	Churchill, Roosevelt	1. Plans for D-Day. 2. Transfer of naval forces for war against Japan and post-war economic matters.
Moscow	October 1944	Churchill, Stalin	Post-war spheres of influence in the Balkans
Yalta	February 1945	Churchill, Roosevelt, Stalin	USSR agreed to enter war against Japan; USSR agreed to creation of UNO; agreement on post-war Polish boundaries and on 'democratic' governments in east Europe.
San Francisco	April/June 1945	Representatives of 50 states	Structure of United Nations Organization agreed and Charter drafted.
Potsdam	July/August 1945	Churchill (replaced by Attlee), Stalin, Truman	Arrangements for Allied control of Germany; Stalin told about atomic bomb.

© Oxford University Press

Unit 19 The Price of World War Two

The total monetary cost (£ millions)

Capitalized value of human life → 47,500

Loss of production ← 62,500

£ 413,250

Property losses → 26,500

Government expenditure ← 276,750

land sea

(Total WW1 75,077)

European dwellings destroyed
(% of pre-war dwellings)

Poland	21·5
Greece	20·7
Netherlands	7·8
France	7·6
Great Britain	6·5
Belgium	6·2
Italy	4·9
Hungary	3·9
Norway	3·6
Czechoslovakia	3·4

The numbers of war dead
(thousands)

(after A.J.P. Taylor)

1	Denmark
5	Luxembourg
10	Norway
20	Bulgaria
84	Finland
88	Belgium
160	Greece
210	Netherlands
334	Austria
365	Czechoslovakia
388	Great Britain
406	USA
410	Italy
420	Hungary
460	Romania
600	France
1,219	Japan
1,700	Yugoslavia
2,200	China
4,200	Germany
4,320	Poland
20,000	USSR

Total: 37,600 (Total WW1: 17,000)

Moneys spent by the Allied and Axis governments (£ thousand million)

Allied and neutral powers

84·5	USA
48·0	USSR
28·0	Great Britain
4·0	Canada
3·75	France
1·25	South America
0·75	Belgium
0·25	Poland
0·25	Netherlands
0·25	Czechoslovakia
0·25	Others/neutral

Total: 171·25

Axis powers

68	Germany
23·5	Italy
14	Japan

Total: 105·5

Moneys advanced to the allies by Great Britain, South America and the USA
(£ thousand million)

USA 1·2
USSR
China 0·4
0·30
2·78
7·9
Great Britain
0·30
0·11 France
South America
Others 0·4 0·1

From Great Britain (Total 1·9)

From South America and the United States (Total 11·59)

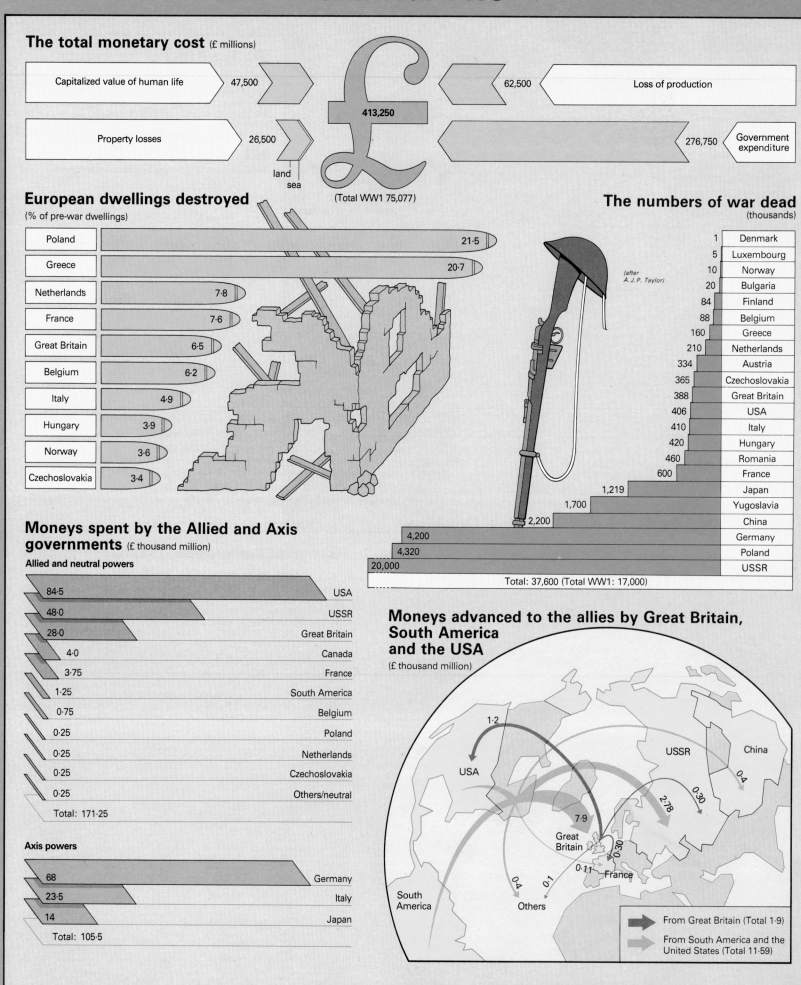

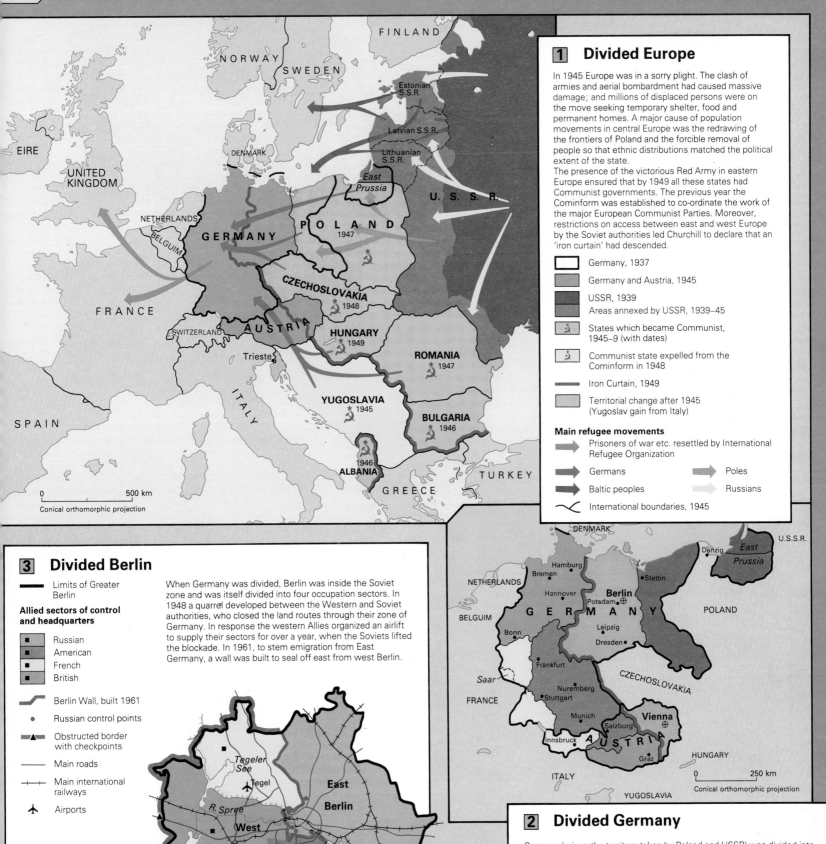

1 Divided Europe

In 1945 Europe was in a sorry plight. The clash of armies and aerial bombardment had caused massive damage; and millions of displaced persons were on the move seeking temporary shelter, food and permanent homes. A major cause of population movements in central Europe was the redrawing of the frontiers of Poland and the forcible removal of people so that ethnic distributions matched the political extent of the state.

The presence of the victorious Red Army in eastern Europe ensured that by 1949 all these states had Communist governments. The previous year the Cominform was established to co-ordinate the work of the major European Communist Parties. Moreover, restrictions on access between east and west Europe by the Soviet authorities led Churchill to declare that an 'iron curtain' had descended.

- ☐ Germany, 1937
- Germany and Austria, 1945
- USSR, 1939
- Areas annexed by USSR, 1939–45
- States which became Communist, 1945–9 (with dates)
- Communist state expelled from the Cominform in 1948
- Iron Curtain, 1949
- Territorial change after 1945 (Yugoslav gain from Italy)

Main refugee movements
- Prisoners of war etc. resettled by International Refugee Organization
- Germans
- Baltic peoples
- Poles
- Russians
- International boundaries, 1945

3 Divided Berlin

- ▬ Limits of Greater Berlin

Allied sectors of control and headquarters
- ■ Russian
- ■ American
- □ French
- ■ British

- Berlin Wall, built 1961
- • Russian control points
- ▲ Obstructed border with checkpoints
- Main roads
- +++ Main international railways
- ✈ Airports

When Germany was divided, Berlin was inside the Soviet zone and was itself divided into four occupation sectors. In 1948 a quarrel developed between the Western and Soviet authorities, who closed the land routes through their zone of Germany. In response the western Allies organized an airlift to supply their sectors for over a year, when the Soviets lifted the blockade. In 1961, to stem emigration from East Germany, a wall was built to seal off east from west Berlin.

2 Divided Germany

Germany (minus the territory taken by Poland and USSR) was divided into four zones of occupation in 1945. But the Allies could not agree on a permanent peace treaty. In 1949 the US, British and French zones became the Federal Republic of Germany and the Soviet, the German Democratic Republic.

- Boundary of Germany and Austria, 1937
- Occupied by Poland
- Occupied by USSR

Allied control zones (of Germany and Austria)

Russian	American	French	British

- ⊕ Divided cities
- Iron Curtain, 1949

© Oxford University Press

Unit 20   The Post-War World: United and Divided

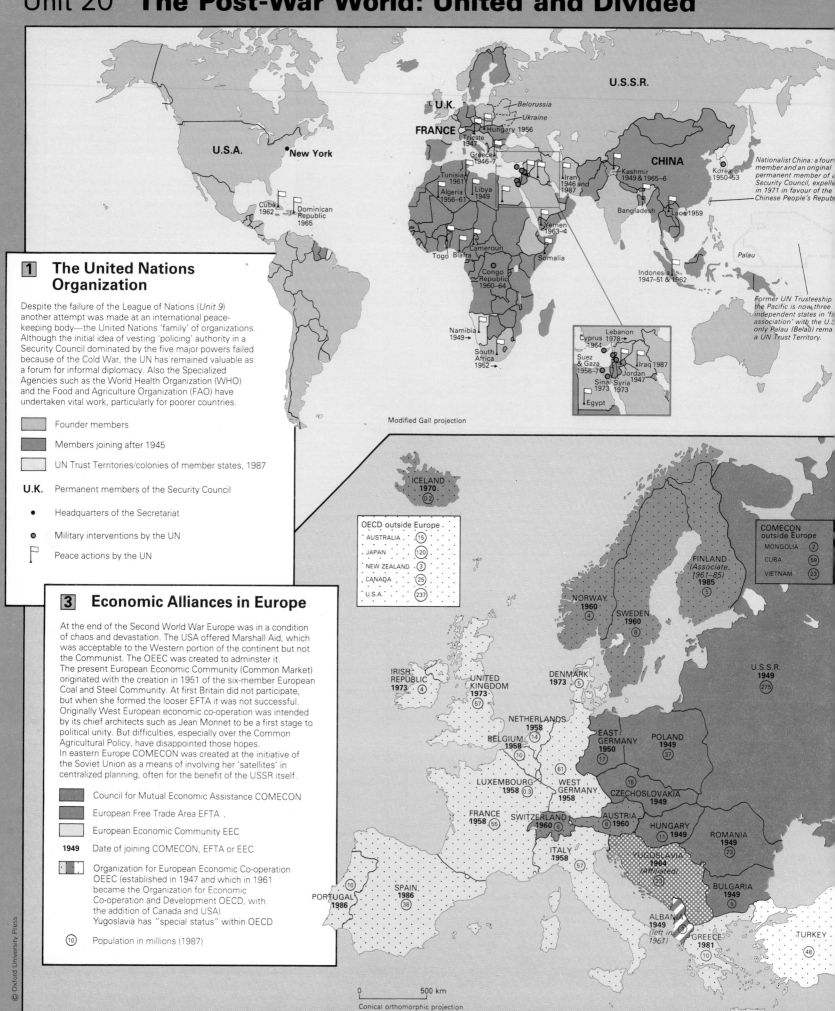

Modified Gall projection

1 The United Nations Organization

Despite the failure of the League of Nations (*Unit 9*) another attempt was made at an international peace-keeping body—the United Nations 'family' of organizations. Although the initial idea of vesting 'policing' authority in a Security Council dominated by the five major powers failed because of the Cold War, the UN has remained valuable as a forum for informal diplomacy. Also the Specialized Agencies such as the World Health Organization (WHO) and the Food and Agriculture Organization (FAO) have undertaken vital work, particularly for poorer countries.

◻ Founder members

◼ Members joining after 1945

◻ UN Trust Territories/colonies of member states, 1987

U.K. Permanent members of the Security Council

● Headquarters of the Secretariat

◉ Military interventions by the UN

⚑ Peace actions by the UN

Nationalist China: a foun member and an original permanent member of Security Council, expelle in 1971 in favour of the Chinese People's Repub

Former UN Trusteeship the Pacific is now three independent states in 'f association' with the U.S only Palau (Belau) rema a UN Trust Territory.

3 Economic Alliances in Europe

At the end of the Second World War Europe was in a condition of chaos and devastation. The USA offered Marshall Aid, which was acceptable to the Western portion of the continent but not the Communist. The OEEC was created to administer it.
The present European Economic Community (Common Market) originated with the creation in 1951 of the six-member European Coal and Steel Community. At first Britain did not participate, but when she formed the looser EFTA it was not successful. Originally West European economic co-operation was intended by its chief architects such as Jean Monnet to be a first stage to political unity. But difficulties, especially over the Common Agricultural Policy, have disappointed those hopes.
In eastern Europe COMECON was created at the initiative of the Soviet Union as a means of involving her 'satellites' in centralized planning, often for the benefit of the USSR itself.

◼ Council for Mutual Economic Assistance COMECON

◼ European Free Trade Area EFTA

◻ European Economic Community EEC

1949 Date of joining COMECON, EFTA or EEC

▨ Organization for European Economic Co-operation OEEC (established in 1947 and which in 1961 became the Organization for Economic Co-operation and Development OECD, with the addition of Canada and USA) Yugoslavia has "special status" within OECD

⑩ Population in millions (1987)

OECD outside Europe
- AUSTRALIA (15)
- JAPAN (120)
- NEW ZEALAND (3)
- CANADA (25)
- U.S.A. (237)

COMECON outside Europe
- MONGOLIA (2)
- CUBA (59)
- VIETNAM (23)

Conical orthomorphic projection

0   500 km

© Oxford University Press

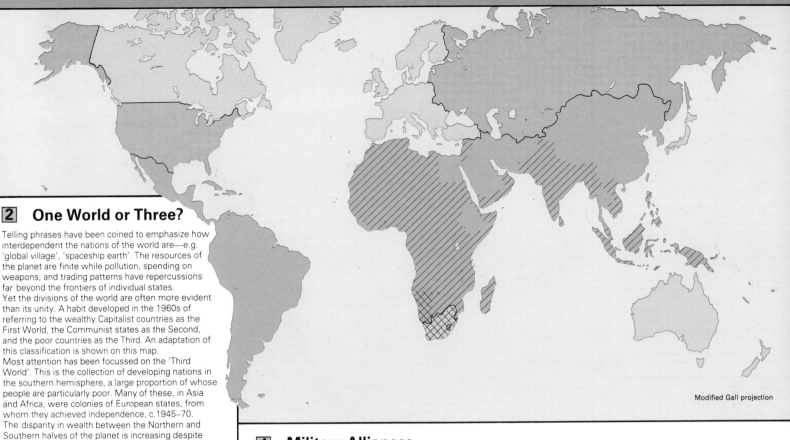

Modified Gall projection

2 One World or Three?

Telling phrases have been coined to emphasize how interdependent the nations of the world are—e.g. 'global village', 'spaceship earth'. The resources of the planet are finite while pollution, spending on weapons, and trading patterns have repercussions far beyond the frontiers of individual states.

Yet the divisions of the world are often more evident than its unity. A habit developed in the 1960s of referring to the wealthy Capitalist countries as the First World, the Communist states as the Second, and the poor countries as the Third. An adaptation of this classification is shown on this map.

Most attention has been focussed on the 'Third World'. This is the collection of developing nations in the southern hemisphere, a large proportion of whose people are particularly poor. Many of these, in Asia and Africa, were colonies of European states, from whom they achieved independence, c.1945–70.

The disparity in wealth between the Northern and Southern halves of the planet is increasing despite attempts by the richer countries to provide financial aid and appeals by the poorer for fairer trading practices (i.e. a New International Economic Order).

```
▨  White/foreign control in Asia and Africa 1945
▧  White/foreign control in Asia and Africa 1980

▨  Superpowers          ⎫ Deng Xiaoping's view of
▨  Developed nations    ⎬ international politics,
▨  Developing nations   ⎭ April 1974.
```

4 Military Alliances

Until the late 1940s states did not engage in military alliances in peacetime. In 1949 the North Atlantic Treaty Organization was created in order to involve the USA in the defence of western Europe against what some statesmen and military men believed was a threat of Communist expansion.

The USA developed the general policy of 'containment', i.e., the prevention of any more states establishing Communist governments. Hence the subsequent alliances in other regions shown on the map. However, from their perspective the Soviet Union saw this process as one of Capitalist encirclement, and responded with the Warsaw Pact. Although post-war Soviet troop levels seemed excessive, historians now doubt that the USSR had any real intentions of military aggression.

— NATO, 1949
— ANZUS, 1951
— SEATO, 1954
— Balkan Pact, 1953–4
— Baghdad Pact, 1955
— Warsaw Pact, 1955

Oblique Aitoff projection

Alliance	Original signatories	History
NATO (1949)	USA, UK, Belgium, Canada Denmark, France, Iceland, Italy, Luxemburg, Netherlands, Norway, Portugal.	1952 Greece and Turkey admitted. 1955 Federal Republic of Germany admitted. 1982 Spain admitted. The forces of France (since 1966) and Spain are not integrated into the military command structures.
ANZUS (1951)	USA, Australia, New Zealand.	Pacific Security Treaty which in 1954 was taken over by SEATO.
SEATO (1954)	USA, UK, Australia, New Zealand, France, Pakistan, Philippines, Thailand.	Manila Treaty for South East Asian defence. Its activities were ended in the 1970s. ASEAN (Association of South-East Asian Nations) formed in 1967 between Indonesia, Malaysia, Philippines, Singapore and Thailand was an alternative non-aligned group designed as an effective form of diplomatic co-operation.
Baghdad Pact (1955)	UK, Iran, Iraq, Pakistan, Turkey.	1959 Iraq left and the Pact was reshaped into CENTO (Central Treaty Organization), more of an economic co-operation. 1979 Iran, Pakistan and Turkey withdrew and the Pact was dissolved.
Warsaw Pact (1949)	USSR, Albania, Bulgaria, Czechoslovakia, German Democratic Republic, Hungary, Poland, Romania.	1961 Albania ceased attending meetings, and was formally expelled in 1968.

1 Britain in the World

Commonwealth territories/members

States which left the Commonwealth
(1972) (with their date of leaving)

 British military and diplomatic involvement

Churchill described Britain's position in the world as being at the intersection of three overlapping circles–having a 'special relationship' with USA; being the originator and having particularly close relations with the Commonwealth; and standing geographically as a part of Europe. However, the past four decades have witnessed an erosion of the 'special relationship'; a steady loosening of Commonwealth ties, especially in terms of trade; and a closer integration with the neighbouring states of Western Europe (*Unit 20*). The official use of the term 'British Commonwealth' instead of or in addition to 'Empire' dates from 1918. The process of decolonization since 1947 has so increased the number of independent members of the Commonwealth that its character has substantially changed. The Queen remains the Head (despite the membership of several republics) and the members are collectively committed to an anti-racialist stance, thus rendering South Africa unacceptable.

Oblique Aitoff projection

KIRIBATI
NAURU TUVALU WESTERN SAMOA
SOLOMON IS. TONGA
FIJI (1987)
VANUATU
PAPUA NEW GUINEA
NEW ZEALAND
AUSTRALIA
CANADA
1950–53 Korea
BRUNEI
MALAYSIA
SINGAPORE
1964–6 Indonesia (confrontation)
1947 (partition and British withdrawal)
BURMA (1948)
BANGLADESH
1948–58 (emergency)
INDIA
BELIZE
BAHAMAS
JAMAICA
IRISH REPUBLIC (1949)
U.K.
1949 Germany (British Army of the Rhine and beginning of NATO)
1973 Brussels (U.K. joining the EEC)
PAKISTAN (1972)
SRI LANKA
ST. CHRISTOPHER-NEVIS
ANTIGUA & BARBUDA
DOMINICA
ST. LUCIA
BARBADOS
ST. VINCENT & THE GRENADINES
GRENADA
TRINIDAD & TOBAGO
GUYANA
MALTA
1954–7 CYPRUS
1944–7 Greece (civil war)
1945–8 Palestine
1956 Suez
MALDIVES
1963–7 Aden (British withdrawal)
THE GAMBIA
SIERRA LEONE
GHANA
NIGERIA
1945–50 Somaliland (administration)
SEYCHELLES
UGANDA
KENYA 1950–54 (Mau-Mau emergency)
MAURITIUS
TANZANIA
ZAMBIA
MALAWI
ZIMBABWE
BOTSWANA
SWAZILAND
LESOTHO
SOUTH AFRICA (1961)
1982 Falkland Islands

The creation of the Welfare State

1942: The Beveridge Report – proposes social insurance from the 'cradle to the grave' as of right.
1946 National Insurance Act – contributions raised from employers, employees and the State to provide Social Services

Education
1944 Education Act – free secondary education for all
1947 School leaving age raised to 15

Poverty
1948 National Assistance Act – payments for the needy

Families
1948 Family Allowance Act – payments for children from the State

Health
1946 National Health Service Act – free Health Service

Unemployment
1946 Unemployment benefit established without 'means test'

2 Troubles in Ireland

132 — Total population (1974)
44% — Catholic population as a percent of total population

— Counties of Northern Ireland (for the purpose of Local Government these were replaced by 26 districts in 1974)

Belfast

The troubles in Northern Ireland (Ulster) have proved so difficult of solution because their roots lie deeply embedded in historical memory and religious conviction. Throughout the centuries English landlords brutally exploited the impoverished Irish peasantry. Then into the predominantly Roman Catholic Ireland in the seventeenth century came Protestant colonists, mainly from Scotland, who settled in the north. At the time of the 'Glorious Revolution' of 1688–9 Catholics supported James II. The Protestants supported William III, Prince of Orange, who remains the hero of the 'Orangemen'. When Ireland became independent in 1921 it was partitioned. However, the boundary was drawn in such a way that the Province of Northern Ireland, though predominantly Protestant, contained a substantial minority of Catholics. This minority has been treated as second-class citizens. Furthermore, many Irish have never accepted the partition at all and created a political party (Sinn Fein) and a military organization (Irish Republican Army (IRA)) to bring about reunification.
The IRA has on occasion resorted to terrorist methods in both Northern Ireland and England to try to force the British government to surrender control over the Province. This has been a particular feature of the period since 1969 when the current 'Troubles' started. Discontent began with protests by the Catholics about the discrimination against them. Tension between the two religious groups in the form of demonstrations and murders escalated. The British government sent troops and suspended the provincial government.

NORTHERN IRELAND
181
138 LONDONDERRY 45%
47%
353
ANTRIM 24%
357
TYRONE 26%
Belfast
FERMANAGH ARMAGH DOWN 309
56 133
53% 44% 24%

0 50 km

Ardoyne Area name
* Sites of riots since 1964
Catholic region

Belfast

Ardoyne
Cliftonville
The Bone
CRUMLIN ROAD
ANTRIM ROAD
M2 MOTORWAY
Shipyards
New Lodge
SHANKILL ROAD
SPRINGFIELD ROAD
Clonard
City Centre
Short Strand
Beechmount
Lower Falls
Ballymurphy
GROSVENOR ROAD
Markets
FALLS ROAD
Sandy Row
River Lagan
Turf Lodge
DONEGALL ROAD
M1 MOTORWAY
LISBURN ROAD
ORMEAU ROAD
Andersontown

0 1km

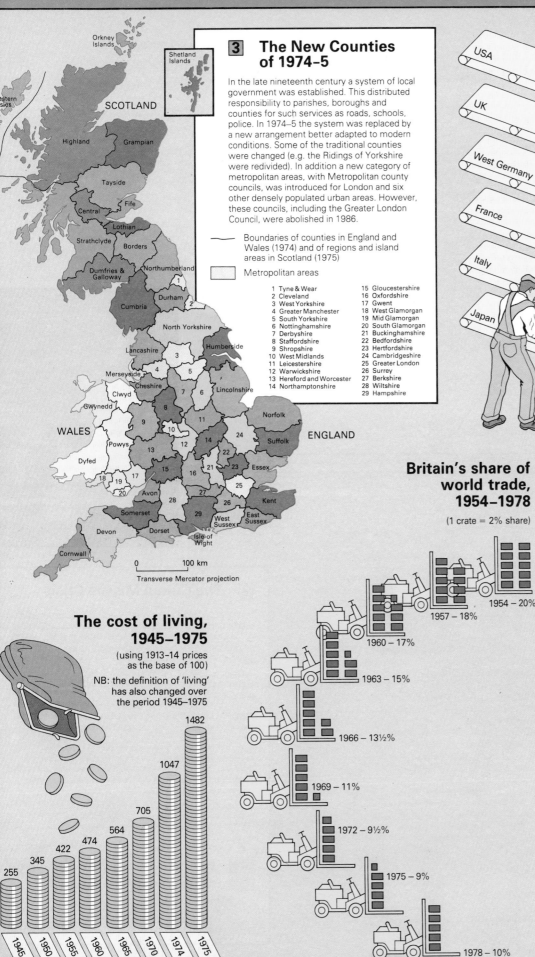

3 The New Counties of 1974–5

In the late nineteenth century a system of local government was established. This distributed responsibility to parishes, boroughs and counties for such services as roads, schools, police. In 1974–5 the system was replaced by a new arrangement better adapted to modern conditions. Some of the traditional counties were changed (e.g. the Ridings of Yorkshire were redivided). In addition a new category of metropolitan areas, with Metropolitan county councils, was introduced for London and six other densely populated urban areas. However, these councils, including the Greater London Council, were abolished in 1986.

— Boundaries of counties in England and Wales (1974) and of regions and island areas in Scotland (1975)

▢ Metropolitan areas

1 Tyne & Wear	15 Gloucestershire
2 Cleveland	16 Oxfordshire
3 West Yorkshire	17 Gwent
4 Greater Manchester	18 West Glamorgan
5 South Yorkshire	19 Mid Glamorgan
6 Nottinghamshire	20 South Glamorgan
7 Derbyshire	21 Buckinghamshire
8 Staffordshire	22 Bedfordshire
9 Shropshire	23 Hertfordshire
10 West Midlands	24 Cambridgeshire
11 Leicestershire	25 Greater London
12 Warwickshire	26 Surrey
13 Hereford and Worcester	27 Berkshire
14 Northamptonshire	28 Wiltshire
	29 Hampshire

Transverse Mercator projection

0   100 km

Output per man-hour in manufacturing, 1974

(using 1961 as the base year of 100 for all countries)

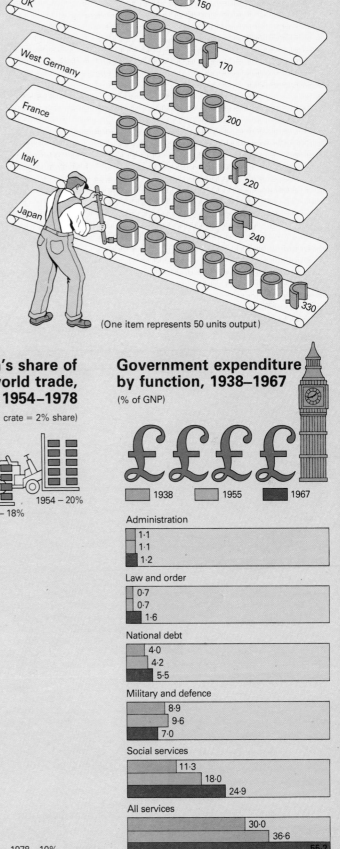

USA — 150
UK — 170
West Germany — 200
France — 220
Italy — 240
Japan — 330

(One item represents 50 units output)

The cost of living, 1945–1975

(using 1913–14 prices as the base of 100)

NB: the definition of 'living' has also changed over the period 1945–1975

1945	1950	1955	1960	1965	1970	1974	1975
255	345	422	474	564	705	1047	1482

Britain's share of world trade, 1954–1978

(1 crate = 2% share)

1954 – 20%
1957 – 18%
1960 – 17%
1963 – 15%
1966 – 13½%
1969 – 11%
1972 – 9½%
1975 – 9%
1978 – 10%

Government expenditure by function, 1938–1967

(% of GNP)

▢ 1938   ▢ 1955   ▢ 1967

Administration
1938	1955	1967
1·1	1·1	1·2

Law and order
1938	1955	1967
0·7	0·7	1·6

National debt
1938	1955	1967
4·0	4·2	5·5

Military and defence
1938	1955	1967
8·9	9·6	7·0

Social services
1938	1955	1967
11·3	18·0	24·9

All services
1938	1955	1967
30·0	36·6	55·2

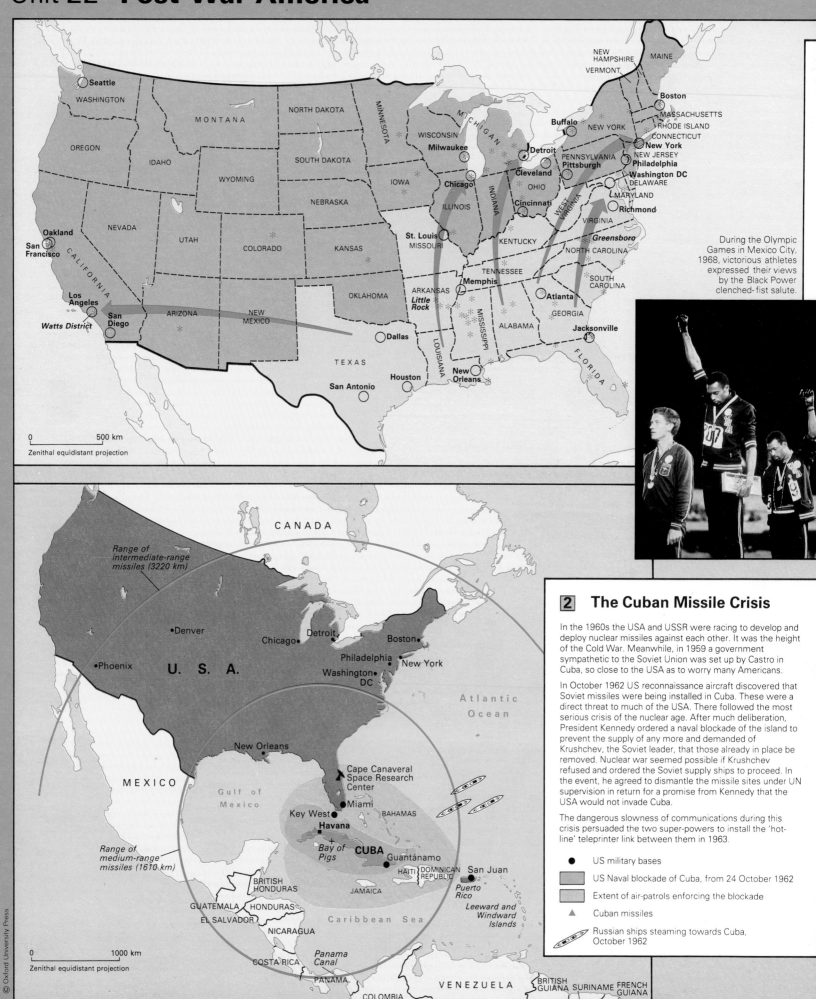

Seattle
WASHINGTON
MONTANA
NORTH DAKOTA
OREGON
IDAHO
WYOMING
SOUTH DAKOTA
MINNESOTA
WISCONSIN
MICHIGAN
Milwaukee
NEW HAMPSHIRE
VERMONT
MAINE
Boston
MASSACHUSETTS
RHODE ISLAND
CONNECTICUT
New York
NEW JERSEY
Philadelphia
Buffalo
NEW YORK
Detroit
Cleveland
Pittsburgh
PENNSYLVANIA
Washington DC
DELAWARE
MARYLAND
Richmond
Oakland
San Francisco
NEVADA
UTAH
COLORADO
NEBRASKA
IOWA
ILLINOIS
Chicago
INDIANA
OHIO
Cincinnati
WEST VIRGINIA
VIRGINIA
CALIFORNIA
Los Angeles
Watts District
San Diego
ARIZONA
NEW MEXICO
KANSAS
St. Louis
MISSOURI
KENTUCKY
TENNESSEE
Memphis
Greensboro
NORTH CAROLINA
SOUTH CAROLINA
Atlanta
GEORGIA
OKLAHOMA
Little Rock
ARKANSAS
MISSISSIPPI
ALABAMA
Jacksonville
Dallas
TEXAS
LOUISIANA
New Orleans
FLORIDA
San Antonio
Houston

0   500 km
Zenithal equidistant projection

During the Olympic Games in Mexico City, 1968, victorious athletes expressed their views by the Black Power clenched-fist salute.

CANADA
Range of intermediate-range missiles (3220 km)
Denver
Chicago
Detroit
Boston
Philadelphia
New York
Washington DC
U.S.A.
Phoenix
Atlantic Ocean
MEXICO
Gulf of Mexico
New Orleans
Cape Canaveral Space Research Center
Miami
BAHAMAS
Key West
Havana
Bay of Pigs
CUBA
Guantánamo
HAITI
DOMINICAN REPUBLIC
San Juan
Puerto Rico
Range of medium-range missiles (1610 km)
BRITISH HONDURAS
JAMAICA
Leeward and Windward Islands
GUATEMALA
HONDURAS
EL SALVADOR
NICARAGUA
Caribbean Sea
COSTA RICA
Panama Canal
PANAMA
VENEZUELA
COLOMBIA
BRITISH GUIANA
SURINAME
FRENCH GUIANA

0   1000 km
Zenithal equidistant projection

© Oxford University Press

2 The Cuban Missile Crisis

In the 1960s the USA and USSR were racing to develop and deploy nuclear missiles against each other. It was the height of the Cold War. Meanwhile, in 1959 a government sympathetic to the Soviet Union was set up by Castro in Cuba, so close to the USA as to worry many Americans.

In October 1962 US reconnaissance aircraft discovered that Soviet missiles were being installed in Cuba. These were a direct threat to much of the USA. There followed the most serious crisis of the nuclear age. After much deliberation, President Kennedy ordered a naval blockade of the island to prevent the supply of any more and demanded of Krushchev, the Soviet leader, that those already in place be removed. Nuclear war seemed possible if Krushchev refused and ordered the Soviet supply ships to proceed. In the event, he agreed to dismantle the missile sites under UN supervision in return for a promise from Kennedy that the USA would not invade Cuba.

The dangerous slowness of communications during this crisis persuaded the two super-powers to install the 'hot-line' teleprinter link between them in 1963.

● US military bases

US Naval blockade of Cuba, from 24 October 1962

Extent of air-patrols enforcing the blockade

▲ Cuban missiles

Russian ships steaming towards Cuba, October 1962

1 Race Relations in the USA

☐ Former 'slave states'

◯ Cities with a large black/negro population

➤ Black/negro migration to major urban centres

✳ Major racial riots/incidents

The history of race relations in the USA has raised some of the most fundamental social and political questions. The very country was founded on the proposition that all men are created free and equal; yet not until nearly a century after the Declaration of Independence was slavery abolished. Even so, people's prejudices cannot be abolished by laws.

The slaves were emancipated during the Civil War and immediately thereafter the Fourteenth and Fifteenth Amendments to the Constitution gave Blacks equal civil and political rights with Whites. In practice, however, widespread discrimination persisted. Various devices were used to prevent Blacks from voting; public places like restaurants, buses and schools were segregated; few Blacks were able to obtain good jobs; some suffered violence at the hands of racist organizations like the Ku Klux Klan. Matters came to a head in the 1950s and 1960s.

During that period a number of movements came into prominence to improve the conditions of the Blacks. Some Black Nationalists rejected much of what the USA stood for, including Christianity. Less radical was the Civil Rights movement and its leader, the Rev. Martin Luther King—they merely claimed their legal rights as American citizens. During the 1960s passions were so inflamed among the black community generally that serious rioting broke out in a number of cities.

The story of the main events is most conveniently started with the Supreme Court decision in 1954 that the segregation of black and white children in different schools was unconstitutional. Three years later President Eisenhower had to send federal troops to Little Rock in Arkansas to enforce desegregation against fierce local white hostility. Then, in 1960, black people, impatient with the lack of progress in desegregation in practical terms, started a 'sit in' campaign in 'white' sections of restaurants and buses, for example. Martin Luther King came to the fore and led a massive peaceful demonstration in Washington in 1963. President Johnson responded with unequivocal civil rights laws. But the assassination in 1968 of M. L. King deprived the black civil rights movement of its most brilliant leader. Also the more radical, violent protests lost their power after the 'long hot summer' outbursts from c.1964–8 in US cities.

Since c.1970 attempts have been made to alleviate the condition of American Blacks by programmes of 'positive discrimination'. These involve the allocation of funds specifically to improve black schools, housing and employment opportunities. Nevertheless, unemployment and poverty remain proportionately higher for Blacks than Whites. Meanwhile, however, the influx of many Spanish-speaking people, especially from Mexico, has created a new 'underclass' even more deprived on average than the Blacks.

Americans often claim they are 'making the world safe for democracy'. This wartime Dutch Nazi poster shows an alternative view.

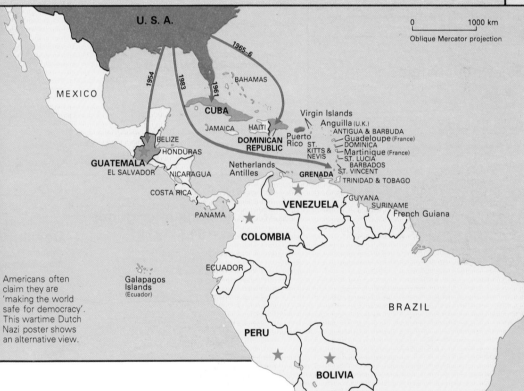

3 Post-war Latin America

Many of the countries of Latin America have suffered from the same three problems: political instability, US interference and poverty. Democratic government has been rare. Individual dictators or rule by military *junta* has been the norm. Violent changes of government, by coup or revolution, have been endemic in many states. Several regimes have used most brutal methods of repression and/or relied upon US support to remain in power. The USA has been concerned to protect its substantial commercial interests in the continent and to counteract Communist influence, a policy partially promoted through the Organization of American States since 1948. US exploitation of the region has been one reason for its poverty. In addition, Mexico, Argentina and Brazil borrowed heavily for development and incurred massive debts in the 1980s.

The first democratically elected Marxist government took office in Chile in 1970. The USA helped to undermine it and it was overthrown in a military coup three years later. Argentina is notable for having had a particularly popular dictator, Perón (President, 1946–58, 1973–74). In 1982 the military government, claiming Argentine right to the British Falkland Islands, engaged in an unsuccessful war for their control. The recent history of Brazil is notable for the clearing of huge areas of the Amazonian forest for agriculture, but with untold harm to the global ecology. Bolivia is a source of Cocaine manufacturing on a massive scale, leading to untold misery in the country and an economy dependent on this illegal trade.

Most Latin American states have unstable economic systems. The situation is exacerbated by a massive population increase—recently averaging 10 per cent for the continent.

➤ US military intervention since 1945

★ Cuban-inspired guerilla movements at work

French poster showing Stalin taking over many countries and threatening France (through the Communist Party).

Major nationalities

(millions, defined according to mother tongue)

	1897	1959
Great Russian	55·6	113·9
Ukrainian	22·4	32·7
White Russian	5·8	6·6
Polish	7·9	0·6
Jewish	5·0	0·5
*Kirgiz/Kaisats	4·0	0·9
Tartar	3·4	4·6
Azerbaizhan	not defined	2·9
*Uzbek	0·7	5·9
Kazakh	not defined	3·6
German	1·8	1·2
Latvian	1·4	1·3
Bashkir	1·3	0·6
Lithuanian	1·2	2·3
Armenian	1·2	2·5
Romanian	1·1	2·2
Estonian	1·0	0·9
Mordvinian	1·0	1·0
Georgian	0·8	2·6
Tadzhik	0·3	1·4
Turkmenian	0·3	1·0
Greek	0·2	0·1
Bulgarian	0·2	0·3
Others		11·9

*NB: Due to redefinitions the 1897 and 1959 figures for Central Asian nationalities are not strictly comparable

1 The Soviet Bloc

During the Second World War and its immediate aftermath the USSR acquired territory on her western border and established friendly 'satellite' governments in the states immediately adjacent. The annexed lands were areas lost at the end of the First World War. The satellites were either the forcible extension of Communism or the creation of a defensive buffer against any further aggression from the West—depending on your point-of-view. The integration of East Germany, Poland, Czechoslovakia, Hungary, Romania and Bulgaria into a Soviet bloc has been achieved in several ways. Immediately after the War contact with the West was minimised—hence Churchill's description of an 'iron curtain'. Soviet-style government and secret police systems were created. In 1949 these states were linked economically in the Council for Mutual Economic Assistance (COMECON) and in 1955, militarily, in the Warsaw Pact.

However, living standards in these countries remained low compared with western Europe. These economic difficulties, combined with resentment of the political repression, has led to several outbursts of violent and dramatic hostility (in East Germany, Poland, Czechoslovakia and Hungary). In the Soviet Union itself discontent was suppressed most brutally under Stalin by the labour-camp system. During the generation following his death dissidence and repression were kept in awkward balance. When Gorbachev became Party Secretary in 1985 (then President additionally in 1988) he initiated a very positive programme of liberalisation.

- - - - - Internal USSR boundaries, 1955

⟋⟍ International boundaries by 1955

▨ Lands incorporated into USSR after 1945

▨ Area of Soviet Influence after 1945

⟋⟍ Iron Curtain, by 1955   ⚡ Crisis since 1945

Capital and consumer goods production, 1913–1978

(Per cent of total industrial output)

▨ Capital goods   ▨ Consumer goods

Year	Capital goods	Consumer goods
1913	33	67
1928	40	60
1937	58	42
1940	61	39
1950	69	31
1960	73	27
1969	74	26
1978	74	26

Development of Siberia and Central Asia

(Per cent share of the USSR's population and production totals for the regions east of the Urals)

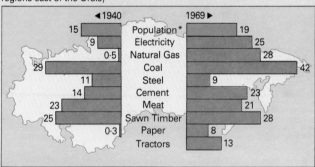

	◀ 1940		1969 ▶
Population*	15		19
Electricity	9		25
Natural Gas	0·5		28
Coal	29		42
Steel	11		9
Cement	14		23
Meat	23		21
Sawn Timber	25		28
Paper	0·3		8
Tractors			13

* The 1913 population of these regions was about 15 per cent of the Empire's population

Birth and death rates, 1872–1978

▨ European Russia

▨ European Russia excluding Caucasus

▨ All territories

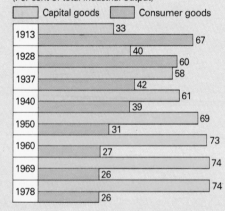

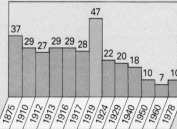

Births per thousand

1872	50
1912	45
1913	47
1916	30
1917	24
1924	43
1928	42
1930	39
1932	31
1935	29

Abortion restricted June 1936

1937	39
1939	36
1940	31
1950	27

Abortion de-restricted 1955

| 1960 | 25 |
| 1978 | 18 |

Deaths per thousand

1875	37
1910	29
1912	27
1913	29
1916	29
1917	28
1919	47
1924	22
1929	20
1940	18
1950	10
1960	7
1978	10

NB: Relatively low death rates in the First World War are partly a consequence of lower birth rates

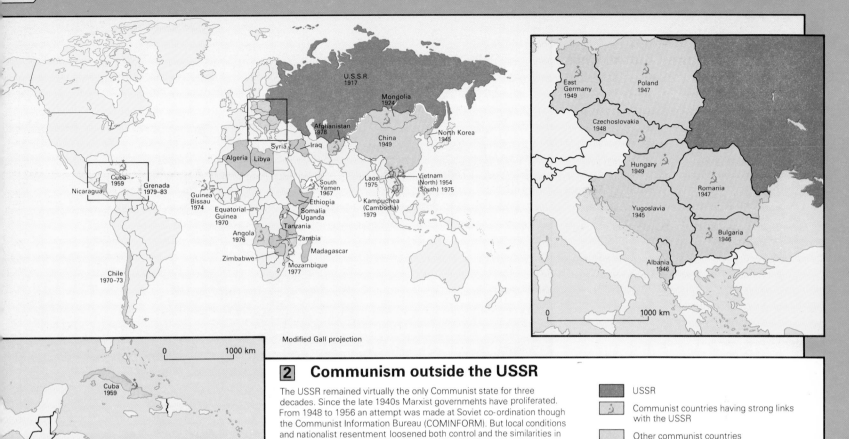

Modified Gall projection

2 Communism outside the USSR

The USSR remained virtually the only Communist state for three decades. Since the late 1940s Marxist governments have proliferated. From 1948 to 1956 an attempt was made at Soviet co-ordination though the Communist Information Bureau (COMINFORM). But local conditions and nationalist resentment loosened both control and the similarities in political ideology and practice. For example, Mao Tse-tung argued the primacy of the peasant over the industrial proletariat as a revolutionary force and engaged in a bitter quarrel with the USSR. The Italian Togliatti argued for 'polycentralism' and Kruschchev conceded that there were 'different roads to Socialism'. African Marxists have particularly had to adapt ideology to local circumstances.

▨	USSR
☭	Communist countries having strong links with the USSR
▨	Other communist countries
1984	Date of change to Communism
〰	Hazardous Sino-Soviet relations
▨	One-party Socialist countries

3 Into Afghanistan

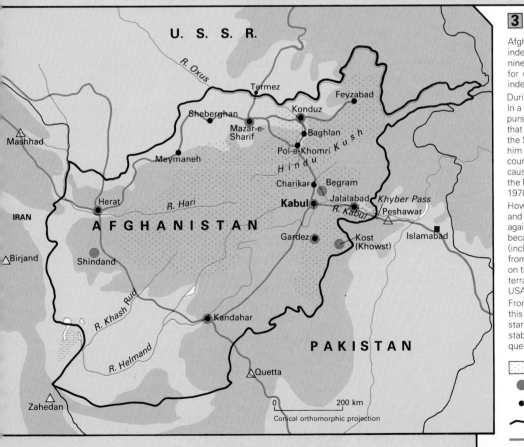

Afghanistan is a mountainous country with a fiercely independent and devoutly religious people. In the late nineteenth century it was the centre of Anglo-Russian rivalry for control of the north-west Indian frontier. It remained an independent state, though under British influence.

During the 1970s there was considerable political instability. In a coup in 1978 a Marxist government came to power. This pursued pro-Soviet and anti-Islamic policies with such fervour that internal opposition to the regime rapidly mounted. In 1979 the Soviet Union installed a puppet prime minister, arranged for him to ask for Soviet support and then sent troops into the country. This extension of Soviet influence in central Asia caused angry international reaction. Several nations boycotted the Moscow Olympic Games and the détente process of the 1970s was undermined.

However, the Soviet Union found itself embroiled in a ruthless and difficult war. Muslim *Mujahidin* organized stout resistance against the government and Soviet forces. However, the war became stalemated. The Soviet forces had superior fire-power, (including tanks and aircraft), controlled the towns and benefited from the bitter feuding between rival rebel groups. The latter, on the other hand, had the advantage of knowledge of the local terrain, (ideal for guerrilla warfare), and military supplies from the USA via Pakistan.

From 1986 Gorbachev sought to extricate the Soviet Union from this quagmire. He installed a more pliant prime minister and started the gradual withdrawal of Soviet troops. The future stability of a tribally and ideologically divided country remained in question.

⠿	Main areas of Afghan guerrilla resistance,1980–82
●	Positions of strength held by the Russians since 1980
•	Principal towns/cities
▬	Border of Afghanistan
──	Main roads
▨	Highland areas
△	Refugee camps

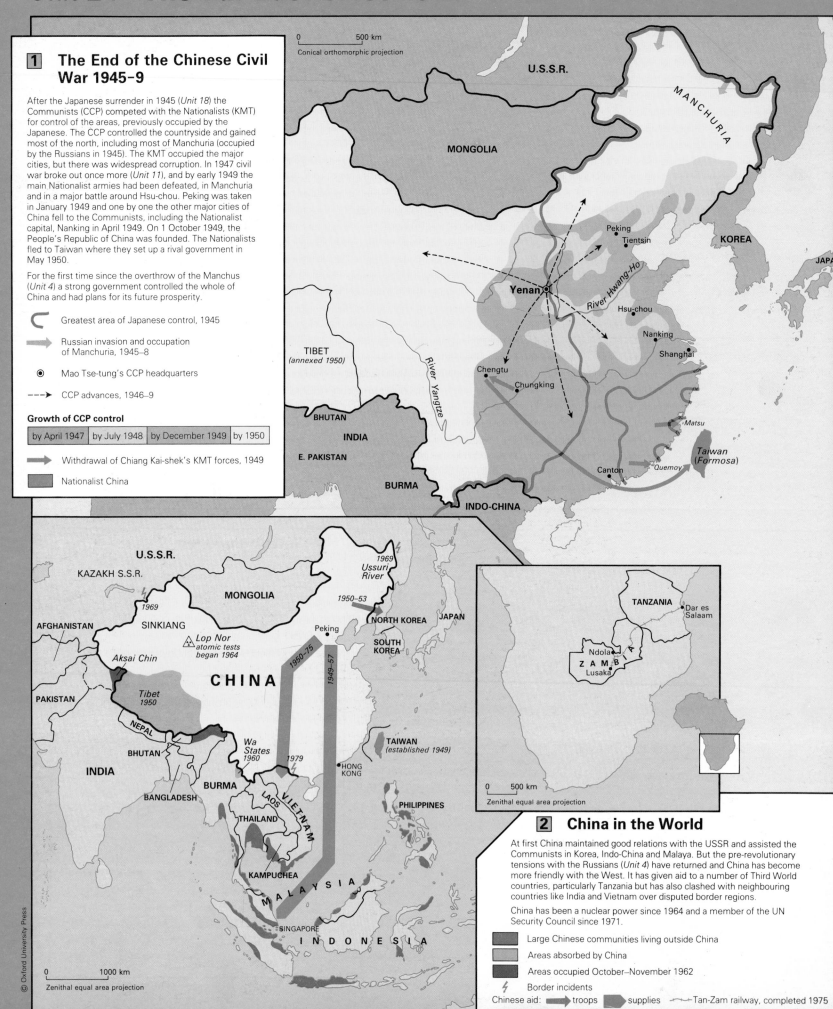

1 The End of the Chinese Civil War 1945-9

After the Japanese surrender in 1945 (*Unit 18*) the Communists (CCP) competed with the Nationalists (KMT) for control of the areas, previously occupied by the Japanese. The CCP controlled the countryside and gained most of the north, including most of Manchuria (occupied by the Russians in 1945). The KMT occupied the major cities, but there was widespread corruption. In 1947 civil war broke out once more (*Unit 11*), and by early 1949 the main Nationalist armies had been defeated, in Manchuria and in a major battle around Hsu-chou. Peking was taken in January 1949 and one by one the other major cities of China fell to the Communists, including the Nationalist capital, Nanking in April 1949. On 1 October 1949, the People's Republic of China was founded. The Nationalists fled to Taiwan where they set up a rival government in May 1950.

For the first time since the overthrow of the Manchus (*Unit 4*) a strong government controlled the whole of China and had plans for its future prosperity.

Ↄ   Greatest area of Japanese control, 1945

⇨   Russian invasion and occupation of Manchuria, 1945-8

⊙   Mao Tse-tung's CCP headquarters

--→   CCP advances, 1946-9

Growth of CCP control

by April 1947	by July 1948	by December 1949	by 1950

➡   Withdrawal of Chiang Kai-shek's KMT forces, 1949

▨   Nationalist China

2 China in the World

At first China maintained good relations with the USSR and assisted the Communists in Korea, Indo-China and Malaya. But the pre-revolutionary tensions with the Russians (*Unit 4*) have returned and China has become more friendly with the West. It has given aid to a number of Third World countries, particularly Tanzania but has also clashed with neighbouring countries like India and Vietnam over disputed border regions.

China has been a nuclear power since 1964 and a member of the UN Security Council since 1971.

▨   Large Chinese communities living outside China

▨   Areas absorbed by China

▨   Areas occupied October–November 1962

⚡   Border incidents

Chinese aid: ⇨ troops   ▬ supplies   ∿ Tan-Zam railway, completed 1975

© Oxford University Press

3 India before Partition

By 1947 the Indian Congress Party had already forced the British to concede major political reforms. Each province had its own government. A large and growing educated middle class and a flourishing industrial base meant that India was well placed for independence except for the crucial issue of the large Muslim minority, which was represented by the Muslim League. The Hindu Congress Party was in control of all but two of the major provinces, the Punjab and Bengal (*map 4*).

—— Boundary of British India in 1939

〜 Province boundaries of British India

Territory under British rule

Princely states

▼ Portuguese territory

▲ French territory

• Major cities

〜 Indo-Pakistan boundary after partition in 1947

4 Independence and Partition

Religious groups before 1947

Predominantly Muslim

Predominantly Hindu. Tamils in Ceylon.

Predominantly Buddhist. Sinhalese in Ceylon.

⋯ Sikhs

Lord Mountbatten, the last British viceroy gave in to Muslim League demands for a separate state, Pakistan, on independence. Partition was pushed through with great speed. There was much bloodshed as Muslims and Hindus fled across the new borders.

—— Border of British India 1939

Independent India, 1947

East and West Pakistan, 1947

States of British India not included in original India or Pakistan after partition, 1947

▲ French bases handed over to India, 1951, 1954

▼ Portuguese territory annexed by India, 1961

⋮ Areas of unrest after partition

⚡ Border dispute (with date)

Refugees:
→ Hindu
→ Muslim
→ Sikh

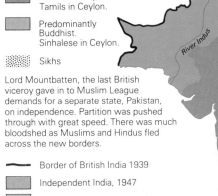

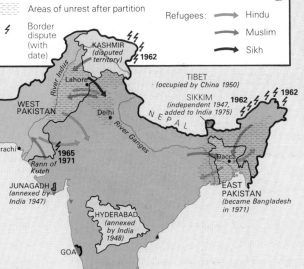

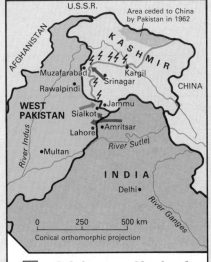

5 Crisis over Kashmir, 1965

In 1947 Kashmir was a predominantly Muslim state with a Hindu ruler who wanted independence. A popular rising against the ruler prompted interference by both India and Pakistan in 1948. The UN arranged a ceasefire. In 1965 the two countries again went to war over the dispute but with no advantage to either side. A similar outbreak of fighting took place in 1971.

—— UN cease-fire line, 1949

⚡ Clashes, August 1965

→ Pakistani advances ⎰ September
→ Indian advances ⎱ 1965

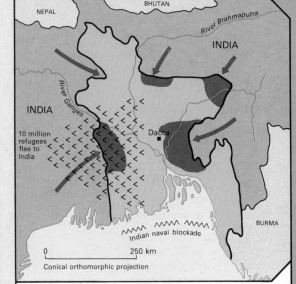

6 The Creation of Bangladesh, 1971

Conflict between the political parties of East and West Pakistan led to demands for greater independence for the East (Bengali). In April 1971 civil war broke out in East Pakistan between Bengalis and the largely West Pakistani federal army. India declared war on Pakistan and forced it to give independence to the Bengalis. East Pakistan became the nation of Bangladesh.

—— Boundary of East Pakistan, 1947

‹‹‹ Bengali refugee movements from April 1971

➡ Indian troop movements, 3 December 1971

Areas held by Indian troops at the time of the surrender of Pakistani army, 16 December 1971

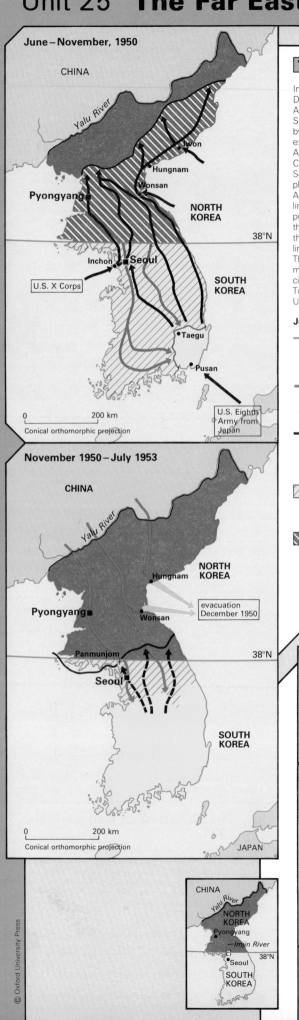

June–November, 1950

CHINA

Yalu River

Iwon

Hungnam

Pyongyang

Wonsan

NORTH KOREA

38°N

Inchon · Seoul

U.S. X Corps

SOUTH KOREA

· Taegu

· Pusan

U.S. Eighth Army from Japan

0 ____ 200 km

Conical orthomorphic projection

November 1950 – July 1953

CHINA

Yalu River

NORTH KOREA

Hungnam

Pyongyang

Wonsan

evacuation December 1950

Panmunjom

38°N

Seoul

SOUTH KOREA

JAPAN

0 ____ 200 km

Conical orthomorphic projection

CHINA

Yalu River

NORTH KOREA

Pyongyang

—Imjin River

38°N

· Seoul

SOUTH KOREA

© Oxford University Press

1 War in Korea 1950–53

In 1945 Korea was divided: a Soviet-supported People's Democratic Republic in the north (capital, Pyongyang) and the American-supported Republic of Korea in the south (capital, Seoul). Tension between them led eventualy to an invasion by North Korean forces, who captured the whole of the south except the area around Pusan within two months.

At this time the USSR was boycotting the UN Security Council (*Unit 20*), so the USA was able to make support for South Korea a UN operation. The US General MacArthur was placed in command of forces from 16 nations, though mostly American. He launched an invasion behind the North Korean lines at Inchon. The North Koreans retreated. UN forces pursued them as far as the border with China, seeming a threat which brought the Chinese into the war. The weight of these Chinese reinforcements forced the UN troops back to a line near the 38th parallel border.

The war was important for a number of reasons. It caused many casualties (nearly 4 million killed), especially among the civilians. MacArthur wanted to invade China, so President Truman sacked him. The war showed the concern of the USA to 'contain' Communism (*Unit 20*).

June–November 1950

——	38th parallel: the border between North and South Korea, 1945–50
→▌	North Korean communist advances, June–September
→▌	South Korean, American and UN troop advances, September–November
▨	Area of South Korea controlled by Communist forces up to 15 September
▧	Area of North Korea controlled by South Korean and UN forces up to 24 November

November 1950 – July 1953

→	Chinese advances, October 1950–January 1951
⇒	UN evacuation
▨	Furthest advance of Chinese troops into South Korea, January 1951
--▶	South Korean and UN troops advances, January–November 1951
━━	Ceasefire line, 27 November 1951 – the area of 'static' or 'limited' war July 1951 to July 1953. This is the present frontier.
+	Location of peace talks 1951–3

Contributors (in addition to the USA) to the UN forces in South Korea

	Army	Navy	Airforce
Australia	2 infantry battalions	various forces	1 fighter squadron
Belgium	1 infantry battalion		
Canada	1 infantry brigade	various forces	1 transport squadron
Colombia	1 infantry battalion	1 frigate	
Ethiopia	1 infantry battalion		
France	1 infantry battalion		
Greece	1 infantry battalion		transport aircraft
Luxembourg	1 infantry company		
Netherlands	1 infantry battalion	various forces	
New Zealand	1 artillery regiment		
Philippines	1 infantry battalion		
	1 company tanks		
S. Africa			1 fighter squadron
Thailand	1 infantry battalion	various forces	air transport
		transport	
Turkey	1 infantry brigade		
United Kingdom	2 infantry brigades	Far Eastern Fleet	2 squadrons of Sunderlands
	1 armoured regiment		
	1½ artillery regiments		
	1½ combat engineer regiments		

Medical care was supplied by Denmark, India, Israel, Italy, Norway and Sweden.

2 Imjin River, 1951

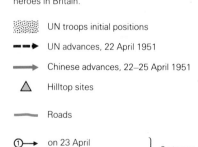

This battle occurred during the UN counter-attack following the intervention of the Chinese. The Chinese, in turn, tried to respond by recapturing Seoul. This plan was thwarted by the stand of the UN troops on the Imjin River. For, despite the victory of the Chinese in the battle, they were held up and sustained heavy losses (70,000 casualties). The brunt of the attack was borne by the Gloucestershire Regiment, all but 39 of whom were killed or captured in the engagement, and who became heroes in Britain.

CHINESE ARMY DIVISIONS

Imjin River

BELGIANS △

Ulster Crossing

ROYAL NORTHUMBERLAND FUSILIERS △

GLOSTERS

ROYAL ULSTER RIFLES

0 ___ 1 km

▒	UN troops initial positions
--▶	UN advances, 22 April 1951
⟶	Chinese advances, 22–25 April 1951
△	Hilltop sites
~~	Roads
①▶	on 23 April
②▶	on night of 23/24 April
③▶	on 25 April

3 stages of UN troop withdrawals

4 | The Vietnam War

After the defeat of the French, Vietnam was divided. The government of North Vietnam was Communist, that of the South was supported by the USA. When the Communists tried to take over the rest of Indo-China the Americans became worried (*Unit 20*) and sent military advisers to help the South Vietnamese army. From 1960 American forces were fighting in South Vietnam and, after the Gulf of Tonkin incident, against North Vietnam also. The war became vicious and the American involvement unpopular in many countries, including the USA itself.

———	International boundaries, 1954
▨	Communist activity in South Vietnam (Viet Cong) and in Laos (Pathet Lao) after 1954
═══	Demilitarized zone created 1954

Communists		**US Forces**	
→	Ho Chi Minh trail	⛴	Naval encounters, Gulf of Tonkin, 1964. US 7th Fleet
•	Towns attacked by Viet Cong in Tet Offensive 29 Jan.– 11 Feb. 1968	○	Major US bases
		⚓	US air raids, from 1965

Area of South Vietnam, Cambodia and southern Laos controlled by Communists during 1975

by January	by March	by 3 April	by 30 April

☐	Neutral countries

3 | War in Indo-China 1945–54

During the Second World War the French colonies of Indo-China were occupied by the Japanese. Although there was a strong nationalist movement under Ho Chi Minh, the French determined to restore their control in 1945. War developed and the French sustained a humiliating defeat when their airborne troops were overwhelmed at Dien Bien Phu.

———	Border of French Indo-China
—·—·	Internal divisions of French Indo-China
—+—+	Main railways
≡≡≡	Areas where risings against French rule occurred before 1945
*	French oppression of the 'nationalist' movement before 1945

Viet Minh (League for the Independence of Vietnam)

▨	Cao Bang, the first area of Viet Minh resistance, 1940
☐	Viet Bac, the Viet Minh core area by 1944
⚑	HQ of Ho Chi Minh from 1944, and source of propaganda broadcasts
⋯⋯	South Delta base area established by the Viet Minh by 1944
•	Cities taken over by Viet Minh in 1945

Allied armies of occupation

◣	Nationalist Chinese	seeking to regain control of the area for France
◣	British	
◣	French	

War 1946–54

⚜	Main battles
- - -	De Lattre fortified defence line, 1951
☐	Area controlled by Viet Minh by the fall of Dien Bien Phu fortress, 1954
▬▬	Armistice line 1954 along 17th parallel creates North and South Vietnam.

5 | The Struggle for South-East Asia

Since 1945 the countries of south-east Asia have gradually gained independence, though not without bloodshed. The greatest violence has occurred in Indonesia and Indo-China. President Sukarno was President of Indonesia, 1945–66. During this time he waged war against Malaysia and massacred about a quarter of a million Communists (mainly Chinese) who opposed his government. More recently, many people have been killed in East (formerly Portuguese) Timor. Cambodia was caught up in the Vietnam war and in 1975 a Communist, the Khmer Rouge, took control. In their attempt to convert the country to a peasant society probably half the population perished. In 1979 Vietnam invaded Cambodia to restore order and created the People's Republic of Kampuchea.

Former status

☐	British colony	▨	Portuguese colony
☐	French colony	▨	Australian territory
▨	Dutch colony	☐	UN Trust territory
☐	US colony		

1961	Date of independence
———	International boundaries as at 1987

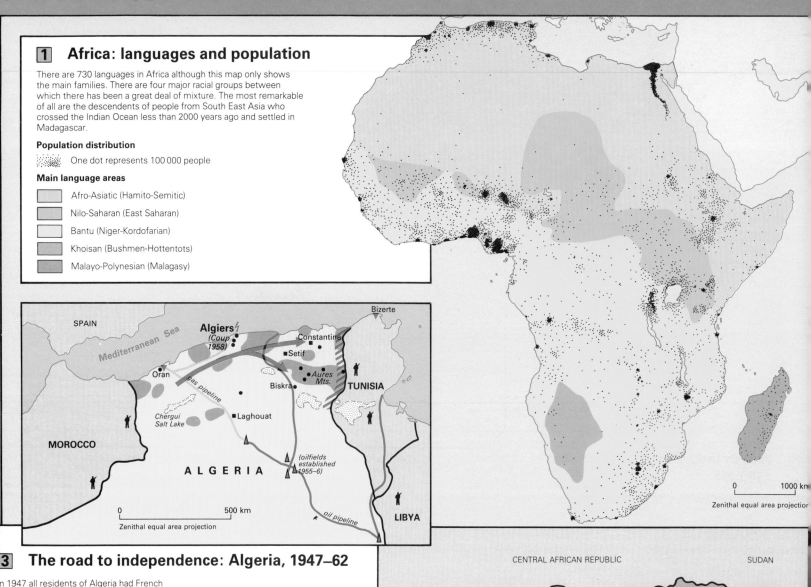

1 Africa: languages and population

There are 730 languages in Africa although this map only shows the main families. There are four major racial groups between which there has been a great deal of mixture. The most remarkable of all are the descendents of people from South East Asia who crossed the Indian Ocean less than 2000 years ago and settled in Madagascar.

Population distribution

⠿ One dot represents 100 000 people

Main language areas

▨ Afro-Asiatic (Hamito-Semitic)

▨ Nilo-Saharan (East Saharan)

☐ Bantu (Niger-Kordofarian)

▨ Khoisan (Bushmen-Hottentots)

▨ Malayo-Polynesian (Malagasy)

3 The road to independence: Algeria, 1947–62

In 1947 all residents of Algeria had French citizenship but power was biased in favour of the European minority.

The uprising on All Saints Day 1954 by the Front de Libération Nationale (FLN) marked the beginning of a long and bitter conflict. Despite success in the cities and the completion of the Morice line, the French army could not destroy the FLN. A coup in Algiers in 1958 brought General de Gaulle to power in France. He began independence talks with the FLN but also launched the Challe Offensive against their strongholds. Meanwhile the many French settlers in Algeria, distrusting de Gaulle, organized a revolt with the help of the French army. Independence came on 3 July 1962.

🏃 FLN training camps

• Centres of All Saints Day uprising, 1 November 1954

▨ Area under FLN control, early 1959

▽ French army bases

▨ Morice line (electric fence and minefield), built in 1957 to block FLN supplies from Tunisia

➡ Challe Offensive, February 1959 to January 1960

4 The road to independence: the Congo, 1960–5

By contrast the Belgian Congo was granted independence under President Kasavubu almost overnight, on 30 July 1960. The trouble began in July 1960 with an army mutiny followed by the secession of the mineral-rich province of Katanga led by Tshombe. The intervention of UN forces prevented civil war, and ended the secession in January 1963. Another uprising, begun in July 1964, proclaimed a 'People's Republic' in Stanleyville. It was put down with Belgian assistance. A coup in November 1965 brought Colonel Mobutu to power.

Areas of the Belgian Congo under the influence of:

☐ Kasavubu/Mobutu

▨ Kalonji

▨ Gizenga

▨ Tshombe

▨ Baluba tribes

Belgian intervention:

▲ 1961

⛱ 1964 (paratroops)

• Centres of rebellion, 1963–4

⚑ UN troop bases established from August 1960

⠿ Maximum extent of rebel uprising, 1964

2   The Progress of Decolonization

The decolonization of Africa happened more quickly than the 'Scramble for Africa' (*Unit 3*). African nationalism spread rapidly after World War Two. The exhausted European nations could not resist demands for the right of Africans to rule Africans. When, in 1947, Britain gave independence to India, there were only four independent countries in Africa. In 1956 France, locked in conflict in Algeria (*map 3*), gave independence to Morocco and Tunisia. By 1966 most of Africa was independent. Only the Portuguese and the white settler communities of Southern Africa refused to give way to the 'wind of change' (*Unit 27*). In some cases independence was followed by internal upheavals (*maps 4 and 5*), boundary disputes (*map 6*) and political quarrels (*Unit 27*).

Independence: by 1950   by 1960   by 1970   by 1980

Independent country ruled by a white minority

1960   Date of independence

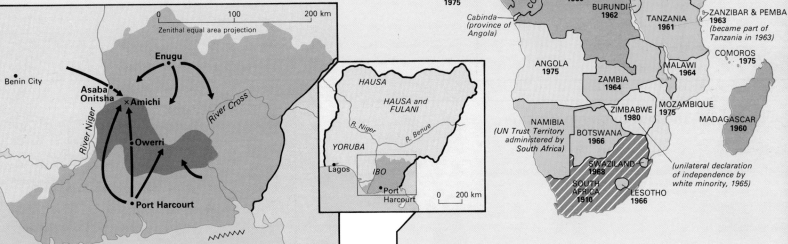

5   Civil War in Nigeria 1967–70

In 1967 Nigeria was a federation of four separate regions. The Ibo were the dominant tribal group in the Eastern Region of Nigeria. Ibo fear of domination by the muslim north led them to declare the Eastern Region the independent country of Biafra in May 1967; Civil war broke out in July. The federal army soon had the upper hand, capturing Enugu, the Biafran capital and Port Harcourt, its main outlet. The Biafrans surrendered in January 1970, but too late to prevent a dreadful famine.

— Boundary of Nigeria

IBO   Main tribes

Biafra in 1967
Biafra in early December 1969

WWWW   Federal blockade

→   Main thrusts of the federal offensive

×   Biafran surrender signed here, 13 January 1970

6   Upheaval in Ethiopia since 1974

Post-war Ethiopia was Africa's only independent monarchy, having experienced only a brief spell of colonial rule (1939–41) (*Unit 14*). Federation with Eritrea took place in 1952 but by 1962 Eritrean separatist groups had become active and were cooperating with similar groups in Tigre province. In addition the drawing of Somalia's boundaries in 1960 had resulted in a continuing feud with Somalia over the Ogaden region where Somali tribes lived. The Ethiopian government failed to resolve these problems, and in 1974 the Emperor Haile Selassie was deposed (⚡) by a committee drawn from all the armed services—the Derg. A period of terror followed during which a new Marxist government established control. Since 1977 support from the USSR and from Cuban troops has helped it contain the separatists and other anti-government guerilla movements.

— Boundary of Ethiopia, 1974

⌁   Province boundaries

⇌   Initial centres of mutiny, 1974

•   Massacres carried out by the Derg

▥   Pockets of resistance to the Derg

✹   Major battles

Territorial claims of separatist movements:

Eritrean
Tigre
Somali
Afar

© Oxford University Press

1 South Africa since 1948

In 1948 the National Party formed a government and has been in power ever since. A succession of leaders— Malan, Verwoerd, Vorster and Botha—have interpreted the party's basic policy of apartheid with varying degrees of rigidity. The policy has had two forms. One, petty apartheid, involved the separation of white and black races in public places and activities, e.g. separate buses, beaches, sports teams. Grand apartheid involved the geographical removal of blacks to Bantustans or homelands, which theoretically were to become independent states.
Apartheid has been bitterly resented by blacks, since in practice it has meant that they have suffered serious discrimination. Campaigning for more just treatment has been organized particularly by the African National Congress (ANC), initially pledged to peaceful methods. However, the government and the security forces responded to demonstrations by the use of considerable force (e.g. at Sharpeville and Soweto) and the ANC was banned in 1961. A more militant wing 'Spear of the Nation' was therefore created for more vigorous action. The ANC leader Nelson Mandela was arrested in 1962 but has become the symbol of black determination for a proper share of power and wealth.

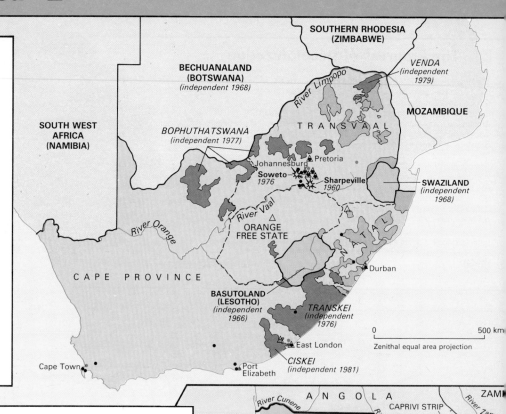

∿ Internationally-recognized boundaries	--·-- Boundaries of provinces of Republic of South Africa
▨ Independent homelands	▨ Other homelands
• ANC 'Spear of the Nation' violence and sabotage, August 1961–January 1963	△ Major strikes, 1973–6
	• ANC violence, 1981–3

2 Namibia—the last colony in Africa?

In 1919 German colonies were allocated to various Allies to be administered as Mandates on behalf of the League of Nations and to be prepared for independence (*Unit 9*). South Africa obtained South-West Africa. However, instead of helping the people in this way, South African governments have tried to make it part of their own country.

In 1960 an independence movement was created— the South-West Africa People's Organization (SWAPO)—and they called their country 'Namibia'. The UN has asked South Africa to arrange elections. Instead, fighting escalated, especially from 1980. South African forces fought SWAPO; Angolan troops supported SWAPO; South Africa invaded Angola; Cuba dispatched troops to support the government in Angola, whose own civil war was made worse by these events.

▬ Boundary of Namibia	Mining centres:
∿ Other international boundaries	▲ copper ▲ diamonds
┿ Railway • Settlement	▲ lead/zinc ▲ uranium
✈ Military air base	▨ SWAPO guerrilla military area

3 Southern Rhodesia becomes Zimbabwe

The progress to independence of the British territories of Northern and Southern Rhodesia and Nyasaland (*Unit 3*) was complicated by the large white population of Southern Rhodesia. Partly to preserve their privileges and partly because of the complementary nature of their economies they were brought together in the short-lived Central African Federation.

When this experiment collapsed Ian Smith, leader of the Rhodesian Front, became prime minister of Southern Rhodesia (now Rhodesia). He resisted British attempts to ensure constitutional arrangements fair to the majority black population in advance of independence and made a Unilateral Declaration of Independence (UDI) in 1965. Attempts to break this rebellion by economic sanctions were abortive. Guerrilla war was therefore waged by the two black nationalist movements (adopting the African name for the land)—Zimbabwe African National Union(ZANU) and Zimbabwe African People's Union (ZAPU).

At first this struggle was difficult because Rhodesia was almost surrounded by white-controlled countries. However, this condition changed with the independence from Portuguese control of Angola and Mozambique in 1975. In 1979 a conference held in London agreed to the transfer of power to a black-dominated government. After hesitations about its leadership, Robert Mugabe of ZANU became prime minister of the independent Republic of Zimbabwe in 1980. However, a period of bitter tension with ZAPU (led by Joshua Nkomo) followed, intensified by tribal rivalries.

By 1987 this rift was sufficiently healed for Mugabe to declare Zimbabwe a one-party state (like so many African countries). This involved also the abolition of the previously guaranteed white seats in parliament.

∿	International boundaries
1964	Date of independence
▬	Boundary of Central African Federation, 1953
▨	Rhodesia declared UDI, 1965
▨	Countries imposing sanctions after 1965
⇢	Oil supply route cut
➡	Continuing trade route with South Africa via new rail link
∿∿∿	British naval blockade
⇨	Advance of ZANU forces, 1972
⚓	'Voice of Zimbabwe' radio station, after 1975
➡	Advance of ZAPU guerrilla units

4 Instability in Africa

It sometimes appears that Africa since independence from colonial rule has been a continent of chronic instability—of *coups d'état*, civil wars and rapid changes from civilian to military government and the attendant bloodshed. On the other hand, when European states were forging their identity in the Middle Ages their record was perhaps no better.

In varying degrees of severity the new states of Africa have faced three major problems, even one of which was bound to strain any political system. One is the artificiality of the boundaries. Most of these were drawn a century ago by the imperial powers in total disregard of the ethnic composition of the territories thus made colonies. Consequently Sudan, Nigeria, and Ethiopia are very large countries, each containing peoples who are racially, linguistically and religiously quite distinct. It is scarcely surprising, therefore, that civil wars have broken out after these states became independent.

Secondly, the imperial powers prepared their colonies for independence with varying degrees of thoroughness. The Belgians and Portuguese were particularly negligent. Therefore, Zaïre, Angola, and Mozambique, for example, had far too few educated people for effective government and administration when the colonial officials withdrew.

A third reason for instability has been outside interference. In particular, South Africa has supported anti-government forces in Angola and Mozambique. Also, American and European firms have retained considerable control of the economies of many African states, a system which the latter have denounced as neo-colonialism. It is possible that the profits enjoyed by these companies have helped to prevent many African states from alleviating the poverty suffered by their people. This poverty also, of course, has environmental causes, especially in the drought-stricken Sahel region to the south of the Sahara desert. Poverty can cause great difficulties for governments.

⌒ International boundaries
▨ States having military rulers, 1987
⌇⌇ Border conflicts
◆ Successful *coup d'état* (with dates)
⚔ Violent insurrection and/or war
▸ Invasion
→ Guerrilla movements

0 ___ 1000 km
Zenithal equal area projection

5 Pan-African Unions

Even before independence a Pan-African movement was created (in the USA in the 1920s); and in 1955 several nationalist leaders attended the Bandung Conference to show their support for the idea of Afro-Asian non-alignment in the Cold War. Then in 1958, a year after the independence of Ghana, Dr Nkrumah called a meeting in his capital, Accra, to encourage the idea of African unity. But in 1961 divisions were already evident. In that year the Casablanca and Brazzaville groups were established, the former favouring radical policies, the latter, moderate and linked to Europe.

However, in 1963 a virtually continent-wide body was established at a meeting in Addis Ababa. This was the Organization of African Unity. Its purposes were to resolve disputes between African states peacefully and to support movements for independence in remaining African colonial territories. Meetings of OAU leaders have been held regularly since, though its influence has declined. One of its achievements has been to secure agreement that the colonial boundaries would remain. This has kept fighting between neighbours on the issue of ownership of territory to a minimum.

Most of the African states were colonies of European states which are now members of the European Community. Some favourable trading terms for the African countries have been negotiated in a series of conventions signed at Lomé since 1975.

⌒ International boundaries
▨ States which took part in the Bandung Conference, 1955
• Sites of Organization of African Unity (OAU) summit meetings since its founding in 1963
▨ Member states of the Lomé Convention, 1975

0 ___ 1000 km
Zenithal equal area projection

© Oxford University Press

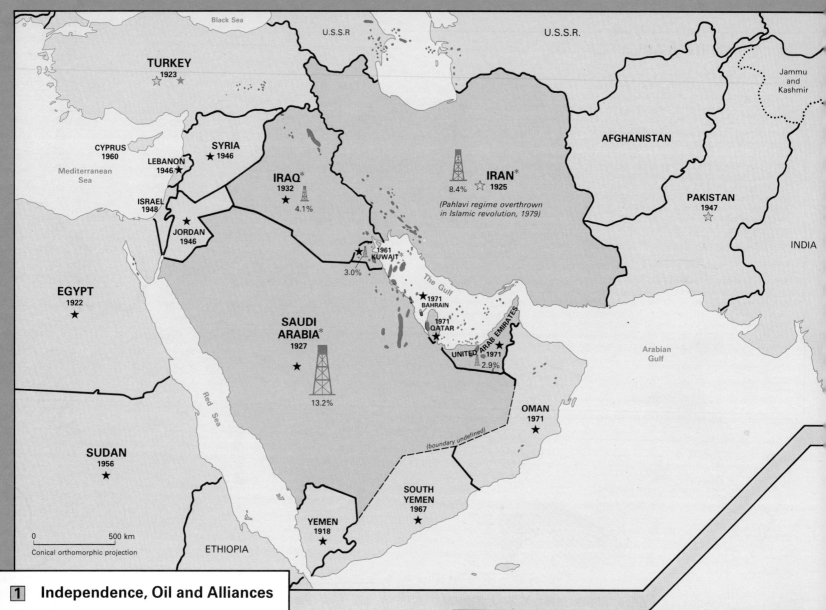

Black Sea

U.S.S.R.

U.S.S.R.

TURKEY
1923 ☆ ★

CYPRUS
1960

Mediterranean
Sea

SYRIA
★ 1946

LEBANON
1946 ★

ISRAEL
1948

IRAQ*
1932
★ 4.1%

AFGHANISTAN

IRAN*
8.4% ☆ 1925

*(Pahlavi regime overthrown
in Islamic revolution, 1979)*

Jammu
and
Kashmir

PAKISTAN
1947 ☆

JORDAN
1946 ★

EGYPT
1922
★

Red
Sea

SAUDI
ARABIA*
1927

★

13.2%

1961
KUWAIT*
3.0%

The Gulf

1971
★ BAHRAIN

1971
QATAR
★

UNITED ARAB EMIRATES
1971
2.9%

INDIA

Arabian
Gulf

OMAN
1971
★

(boundary undefined)

0   500 km
Conical orthomorphic projection

SUDAN
1956
★

YEMEN
1918
★

SOUTH
YEMEN
1967
★

ETHIOPIA

1 Independence, Oil and Alliances

During the nineteenth century most of the Middle East was
under alien control—Ottoman Turk and British. Even when
nominal independence was achieved by some countries after
the First World War, Western influence remained, increased by
the interests of British and American oil companies. The
process of independence proceeded after the Second World
War with the French and British withdrawal from empire. The
failure of the Suez adventure *(map 5)* marked the end of this
phase. The Americans attempted to fill this gap in Western
control. Close friendship with Israel and military alliances
were the main planks of this policy; keeping Soviet influence
at bay and protecting oil supplies were the main motives.
However, the world's thirst for oil provided the oil-rich states
of the area with a powerful economic weapon for protecting
their independence.

— International boundaries, 1978

1967 Dates of independence

★ League of Arab States, 1978

☆ Membership of CENTO
(Central Treaty Organization), 1978

★ Membership of NATO
(North Atlantic Treaty Organization), 1978

Main oilfields

Founder members* and other members of OPEC
(Organization of Petroleum Exporting Countries)

Oil production, as a percentage of world
production, 1978

Jews as a percentage of
the total population of
Palestine 1880–1949

100
90
80
70
60
% 50
40
30
20
10
0
1880 1914 1922 1931 1939 1949

5 Suez and Sinai, 1956

From its very foundation Israel was
subjected to Arab commando raids
across its borders. The most
powerful of Israel's enemies was
Nasser, President of Egypt, 1954–70.
Nasser also frightened and angered
Britain and France in three ways. He
expressed his wish for Egypt to lead
a Pan-Arab union. He bought weapons
from the Communist bloc. He
nationalised the Suez Canal to obtain
funds for building the Aswan Dam.
The Suez Canal has been a vital
communications link and Britain and
France had controlling financial
interests in the company which
operated it. The British prime
minister, Eden, believed that its

nationalisation was an aggressive
act akin to Mussolini's policies and
that Nasser had to be stopped
before he became too powerful.
The British, French and Israeli
governments entered into a plot.
Israel invaded Egypt. Using the
pretext of separating the combatants
to protect the Canal, British and
French forces landed in Egypt.
The result was international uproar
against the invaders. The Soviet
leader threatened a nuclear attack.
The US president refused to
support the pound sterling which
plunged in value. The whole Afro-
Asian world was shocked. The
invaders ignominiously withdrew.

〜 International boundaries

Suez Canal

• Egyptian air bases

→ Israeli attacks,
29 October–5 November

→ Anglo-French air-attacks,
31 October–4 November

• British and French
air bases

→ French naval bombardment,
1 November

▼ Anglo-French invasion,
5 November

© Oxford University Press

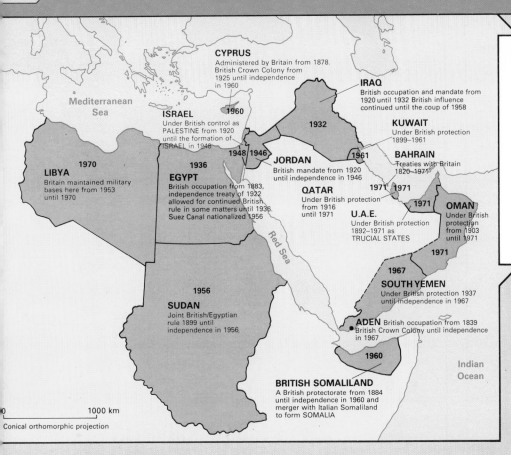

CYPRUS
Administered by Britain from 1878.
British Crown Colony from
1925 until independence
in 1960

IRAQ
British occupation and mandate from
1920 until 1932 British influence
continued until the coup of 1958

1960

1932

ISRAEL
Under British control as
PALESTINE from 1920
until the formation of
ISRAEL in 1948

KUWAIT
Under British protection
1899–1961

1948 1946

1961

BAHRAIN
Treaties with Britain
1820–1971

LIBYA
1970
Britain maintained military
bases here from 1953
until 1970

1936

JORDAN
British mandate from 1920
until independence in 1946

1971 1971

EGYPT
British occupation from 1883,
independence treaty of 1922
allowed for continued British
rule in some matters until 1936.
Suez Canal nationalized 1956

QATAR
Under British protection
from 1916
until 1971

1971

OMAN
Under British
protection
from 1903
until 1971

U.A.E.
Under British protection
1892–1971 as
TRUCIAL STATES

1971

1956

1967

SUDAN
Joint British/Egyptian
rule 1899 until
independence in 1956

SOUTH YEMEN
Under British protection 1937
until independence in 1967

1960

ADEN British occupation from 1839
British Crown Colony until independence
in 1967

1000 km

Conical orthomorphic projection

BRITISH SOMALILAND
A British protectorate from 1884
until independence in 1960 and
merger with Italian Somaliland
to form SOMALIA

Indian
Ocean

2 The British Withdrawal

British interest in the Middle East stemmed originally from the need to protect the route to India—via the Mediterranean, Red Sea and Indian Ocean. However, by 1945 Britain lacked the resources and will-power to sustain her control, especially in the face of militant nationalist demands for independence in the region and the concession of independence to India and Pakistan. British forces suffered particularly violent opposition to their continuing presence in Palestine, Egypt, Cyprus and Aden. British control was rapidly becoming a liability rather than an asset.

On the other hand, the increasing importance of oil supplies and dreams of maintaining some remnants of empire suggested that the effort to retain a presence in the area should be made. Consequently the final decision to withdraw from 'east of Suez' was delayed until the 1960s.

Areas from which the British withdrew, 1932–71

1971 Date of withdrawal

3 Palestine and Israel, 1947–9

The competing demands of Jews and Arabs to have Palestine were too much for Britain, the governing power, to cope with. She passed the problem to the UN, which produced a partition plan. War broke out between the new Jewish state of Israel and neighbouring Arab states. Israel was victorious and gained extra territory.

— Boundary of British mandated territory

UN Partition Plan, 1947

Arab territory

Jewish territory

International territory

Jewish settlement areas

→ Lines of Arab attack, 15 May 1948

0   50 km

Mediterranean Sea
Lebanese
LEBANON
Syrian
Haifa
Galilee
SYRIA
Nazareth
Nablus
Iraqi
Tel Aviv
Samaria
from
Transjordan
Jerusalem
Gaza
Dead
Sea
Beersheba
Egyptian
TRANSJORDAN
Negev
EGYPT

4 Israel after 1949

Israel's first prime minister was Ben-Gurion, 1948–63. During this time Israelis worked very hard to develop their country and build a strong army. Co-operative *kibbutzim* were founded. But the country needed more people: the Law of Return (1950) allowed Jews the right of immigration. $1\frac{1}{2}$ million arrived, 1948–73. But the Palestinian Arabs who remained were treated as second-class citizens.

Israel

West Bank—became part of Jordan from April 1950

▬ ▬ Demarcation lines, 3 April 1949

■ Jerusalem partitioned 1949

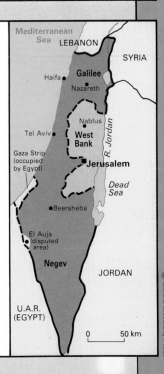

Mediterranean Sea
LEBANON
Haifa
Galilee
SYRIA
Nazareth
Nablus
Tel Aviv
West
Bank
Gaza Strip
(occupied
by Egypt)
Jerusalem
Dead
Sea
Beersheba
El Auja
(disputed
area)
Negev
JORDAN
U.A.R.
(EGYPT)
0   50 km

Nicosia
CYPRUS
Limassol

Mediterranean
Sea

SYRIA

from
Malta

British

British

LEBANON

Haifa

French

Tel Aviv

ISRAEL

R. Jordan

Jerusalem

Dead
Sea

Port
Said

JORDAN

Ismailia

Cairo

Suez

E G Y P T

Gulf of Suez

Gulf of Aqaba

SAUDI
ARABIA

0   200 km

Conical orthomorphic projection

Red Sea

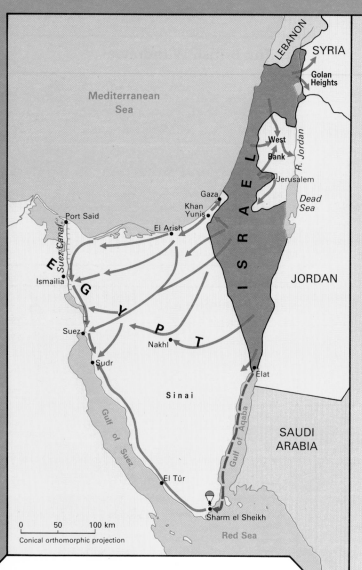

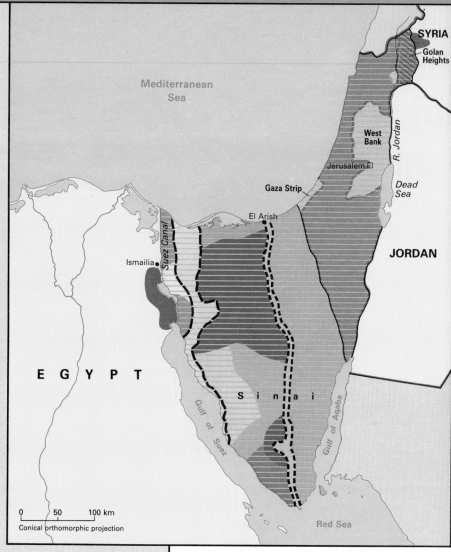

1 The Six Day War, 1967

After the Suez invasion *(Unit 28, map 5)* a UN force guarded the Israel–Egypt border. However, tension remained. In 1967 Nasser ordered the UN troops to withdraw and closed the Gulf of Aqaba to Israeli ships (they were already denied use of the Suez Canal). The Israelis decided to strike. They succeeded with lightning speed. They destroyed the bulk of the military aircraft of Egypt, Syria, Jordan and Iraq. Their armies took Sinai from Egypt, the West Bank from Jordan and the Golan Heights from Syria within six days.

Israel now felt much more secure: her armed forces seemed invincible; the extra territory made the tiny state less vulnerable to surprise attack; and the whole of the holy city of Jerusalem was now in Jewish hands. Nevertheless, the very success raised problems. The Arab states, smarting from the humiliation, renovated their armed forces. Secondly, there was the Palestinian issue. During the 1948–9 war many Palestinian Arabs became refugees rather than submit to Jewish rule. Large numbers settled in camps in the Gaza Strip and the West Bank (incorporated into Jordan). These Palestinians now came under Israeli rule. The proportion of Jews in the population of this Greater Israel consequently declined. Also, the hopes of the Palestinians for a state of their own seemed dashed. The Palestine Liberation Organization, formed in 1964, now turned, in desperation, to terrorist tactics. The PLO and their leader, Yasser Arafat, refused to recognise the right of Israel to exist; Israel refused to negotiate.

Legend for map 1:
- International boundary, 1949
- Israel
- → Israeli attacks 5–8 June
- ⇢ Naval force
- Airborne attack

2 Israel after 1967

Legend for map 2:
- International boundary
- Israel before the war
- Conquests during the war

3 Israel since the Yom Kippur War, 1973

In 1973 Egypt suddenly attacked Israel during the religious festival of Yom Kippur. The two sides were now evenly matched and fought each other to a standstill. In 1978 US President Carter invited Prime Minister Begin of Israel and President Sadat of Egypt to Camp David in the USA. Israel agreed to withdraw from Sinai; but the fate of the Palestinians was left vague. Indeed, Begin had no intention of surrendering the West Bank (which he called by the biblical names of Judaea and Samaria) and encouraged Jewish settlements there.

- International boundaries, 1949
- Israel in 1973

Land captured in Yom Kippur War

- By Israel
- By Egypt
- ▰▰▰ Front lines, March 1979. These had defined the buffer zone from September 1975 to April 1979.

Phased Israeli withdrawal (April 1979–April 1982) by:

May 1979	July 1979	September 1979	November 1979	January 1980

- ▰▰▰ Buffer Zone January 1980
- by April 1982
- Annexation of Golan Heights, 1981
- International boundary, April 1982
- Land claimed by Palestinians

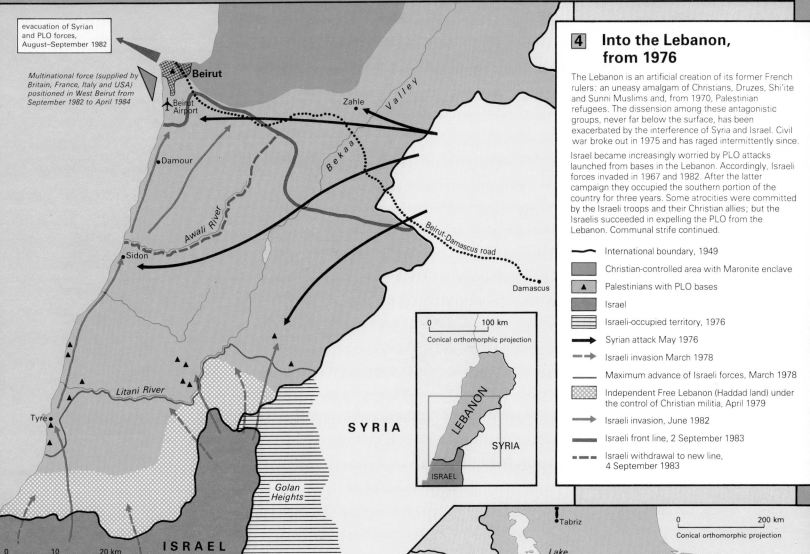

evacuation of Syrian and PLO forces, August–September 1982

Multinational force (supplied by Britain, France, Italy and USA) positioned in West Beirut from September 1982 to April 1984

Beirut
↑ Beirut Airport
• Damour
Zahle
Bekaa Valley
Awali River
• Sidon
Beirut-Damascus road
Damascus
Litani River
• Tyre
SYRIA
Golan Heights
ISRAEL

0   10   20 km
Conical orthomorphic projection

0   100 km
Conical orthomorphic projection

LEBANON
SYRIA
ISRAEL

4 Into the Lebanon, from 1976

The Lebanon is an artificial creation of its former French rulers: an uneasy amalgam of Christians, Druzes, Shi'ite and Sunni Muslims and, from 1970, Palestinian refugees. The dissension among these antagonistic groups, never far below the surface, has been exacerbated by the interference of Syria and Israel. Civil war broke out in 1975 and has raged intermittently since.

Israel became increasingly worried by PLO attacks launched from bases in the Lebanon. Accordingly, Israeli forces invaded in 1967 and 1982. After the latter campaign they occupied the southern portion of the country for three years. Some atrocities were committed by the Israeli troops and their Christian allies; but the Israelis succeeded in expelling the PLO from the Lebanon. Communal strife continued.

— International boundary, 1949

▨ Christian-controlled area with Maronite enclave

▲ Palestinians with PLO bases

▨ Israel

▤ Israeli-occupied territory, 1976

➤ Syrian attack May 1976

╌➤ Israeli invasion March 1978

— Maximum advance of Israeli forces, March 1978

▨ Independent Free Lebanon (Haddad land) under the control of Christian militia, April 1979

➤ Israeli invasion, June 1982

▬ Israeli front line, 2 September 1983

╍ Israeli withdrawal to new line, 4 September 1983

5 The Gulf War, 1980–88

In 1979 a revolution occurred in Iran in which the pro-American Shah was deposed. The fundamentalist Shi'ite Ayatollah Khomeini became the Iranian leader and demanded and encouraged strict adherence to the Muslim way of life.
The following year Iraq attacked Iran. There were two main causes of tension between the two states. One was the control of the vital Shatt al Arab waterway. The other was the position of the minority Shia population in Iraq. President Saddam Hussain feared they would be disaffected towards his government by events in neighbouring Iran. The war was fought with exceeding ferocity. Raw Iranian recruits, believing in the posthumous reward of martyrdom, were sacrificed in huge numbers against the better-equipped Iraqis. The Iraqis, in turn,

violated international law by using poison gas. In the meantime, the conflict became an issue of considerable international interest. The economies of the combatants depended on the export of oil. Tankers therefore became targets. But many belonged to other nations. Several nations, most conspicuously the Americans, ultimately dispatched escorting naval squadrons to defend these vessels and keep open the vital Gulf shipping lanes. The Americans had other motives too. They were fearful of any extension of Soviet influence in the area, particularly in the light of their involvement in Afghanistan *(Unit 23 map 3)*. They were also more hostile to Iran than to Iraq because of the former's treatment of American embassy personnel at the time of the revolution. A truce of exhaustion was agreed through UN mediation in 1988.

— International boundaries

▨ Iraq

➤ Main Iraqi attacks, September 1980

▮ Main Iraqi air strikes

▨ Iraqi-occupied territory by end of 1980

▨ Iran

➤ Iranian counter-attacks, April–May 1982

▮ Iranian air strikes

∴ Oilfields

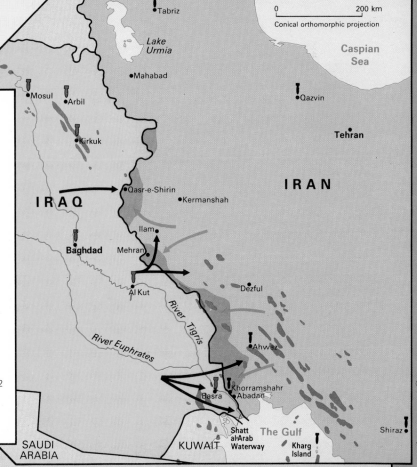

• Tabriz
Lake Urmia
• Mahabad
Caspian Sea
• Mosul
• Arbil
• Qazvin
• Kirkuk
Tehran
IRAQ
Qasr-e-Shirin
• Kermanshah
IRAN
Baghdad
Ilam •
Mehran •
Al Kut •
River Tigris
• Dezful
River Euphrates
• Ahwaz
Khorramshahr
Basra • Abadan
The Gulf
• Shiraz
SAUDI ARABIA
KUWAIT
Shatt al Arab Waterway
Kharg Island

© Oxford University Press

Unit 30 Time Chart

| | 1900 | 1910 | 1920 | 1930 | 1940 |

Europe

- **1900** King Umberto of Italy assassinated
- **1904** France and Britain sign the 'Entente Cordiale'
- **1906** HMS *Dreadnought* launched. Naval arms race begins
- **1907** Anglo-Russian Entente
- **1910** Revolution in Portugal, King overthrown
- **1911** Agadir Crisis. Tension between Britain and Germany
- **1912–13** Balkan Wars
- **1914** Assassination of Archduke Ferdinand. WORLD WAR 1 begins
- **1916** Easter Rebellion in Ireland
- **1916** Battles of Somme and Jutland. Defence of Verdun
- **1918** End of WORLD WAR 1
- **1920** League of Nations founded
- **1920** Civil War in Ireland
- **1922** Mussolini's march on Rome
- **1923** Hitler attempts *putsch* in Munich
- **1923** Inflation in Germany
- **1923** French occupation of Ruhr
- **1925** Locarno Treaties. Rhineland demilitarized
- **1926** General Strike in Britain
- **1933** Hitler becomes Chancellor of Germany
- **1935** Saar returned to Germany
- **1936–39** Civil War in Spain
- **1936** Germany reoccupies Rhineland
- **1938** Germans march into Austria Munich agreement
- **1939** Germany invades Poland WORLD WAR 2 begins

U.S.S.R.

- **1905** Revolution in Russia
- **1914** Russia enters war
- **1917** Revolutions in Russia. Bolsheviks seize control
- **1918** Treaty of Brest-Litovsk Russia out of war
- **1919/22** Civil war in Russia
- **1923** USSR proclaimed
- **1924** Death of Lenin Stalin takes control
- **1927** Trotsky expelled from Communist Party
- **1928** Stalin's first 5 year plan
- **1932/34** Widespread famines
- **1935/38** Stalin's purges
- **1939** USSR signs non-aggression pact with Germany

Africa

- **1902** Boer War ends
- **1910** The Union of South Africa formed
- **1912** Founding of African National Congress
- **1919** German colonies mandated to Britain, France, South Africa and Belgium
- **1930** Haile Selassie becomes Emperor of Ethiopia
- **1935–6** Italians conquer Ethiopia

Asia and Australasia

- **1900** Boxer Rebellion in China
- **1901** Australia becomes a Commonwealth
- **1904–05** Russo-Japanese War
- **1907** New Zealand becomes a Dominion
- **1912** Chinese Republic proclaimed under Sun Yat-sen
- **1915** Allies fail to capture Dardanelles Heavy ANZAC losses
- **1919** Massacre at Amritsar
- **1919** Japan acquires North Pacific Islands from Germany
- **1923** Turkey becomes a republic under Ataturk
- **1925** Death of Sun Yat-sen. Chiang Kai-shek in control
- **1931** Japanese occupy Manchuria
- **1937** Japan invades China

The Americas

- **1901** US President McKinley assassinated
- **1912** US Marines enter Cuba
- **1914** Panama Canal opened
- **1917** USA enters war
- **1919** Prohibition in USA
- **1929** Wall Street crash
- **1930** Right-wing dictatorships in Brazil and Argentina
- **1932** Roosevelt elected President. New Deal begins
- **1933** Prohibition ends in USA

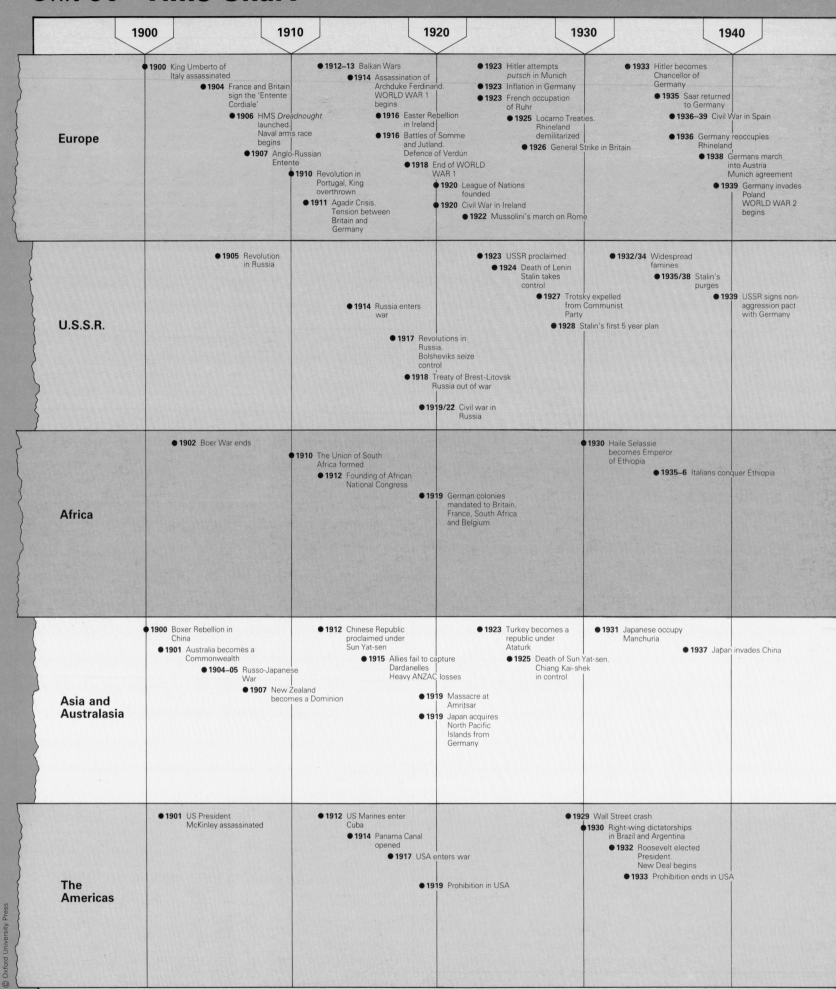

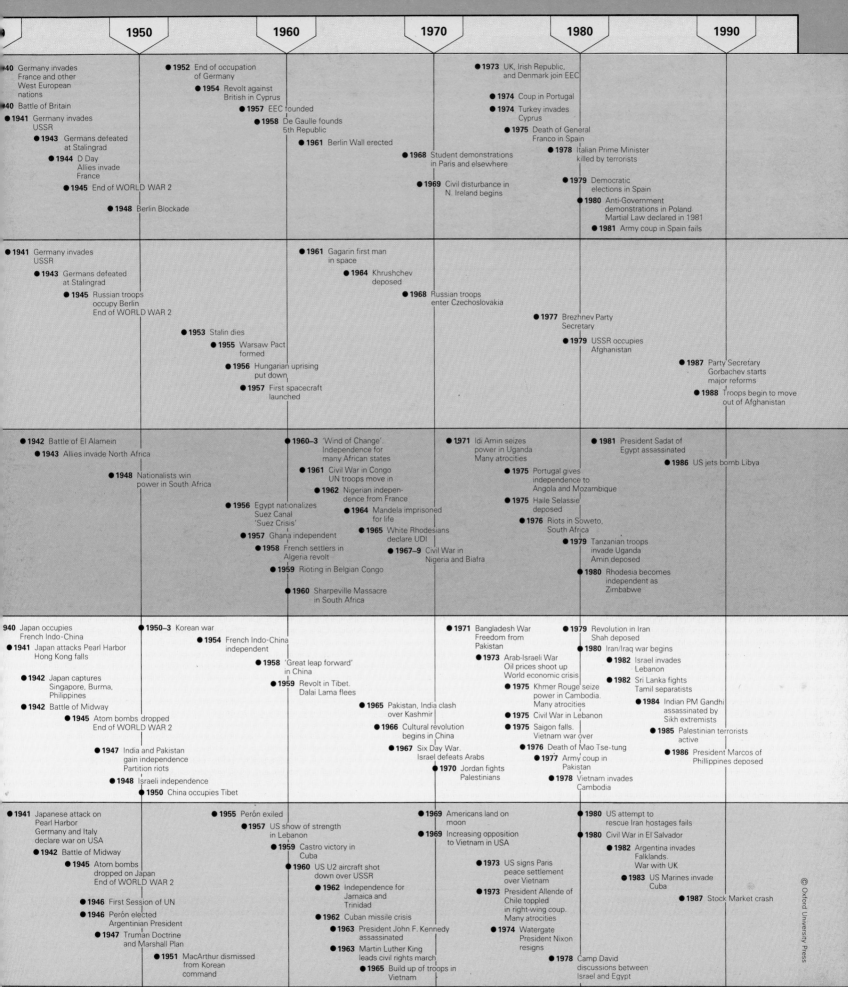

Timeline: 1940–1990

Western Europe

- 1940 Germany invades France and other West European nations
- 1940 Battle of Britain
- 1941 Germany invades USSR
- 1943 Germans defeated at Stalingrad
- 1944 D Day Allies invade France
- 1945 End of WORLD WAR 2
- 1948 Berlin Blockade
- 1952 End of occupation of Germany
- 1954 Revolt against British in Cyprus
- 1957 EEC founded
- 1958 De Gaulle founds 5th Republic
- 1961 Berlin Wall erected
- 1968 Student demonstrations in Paris and elsewhere
- 1969 Civil disturbance in N. Ireland begins
- 1973 UK, Irish Republic, and Denmark join EEC
- 1974 Coup in Portugal
- 1974 Turkey invades Cyprus
- 1975 Death of General Franco in Spain
- 1978 Italian Prime Minister killed by terrorists
- 1979 Democratic elections in Spain
- 1980 Anti-Government demonstrations in Poland. Martial Law declared in 1981
- 1981 Army coup in Spain fails

USSR

- 1941 Germany invades USSR
- 1943 Germans defeated at Stalingrad
- 1945 Russian troops occupy Berlin End of WORLD WAR 2
- 1953 Stalin dies
- 1955 Warsaw Pact formed
- 1956 Hungarian uprising put down
- 1957 First spacecraft launched
- 1961 Gagarin first man in space
- 1964 Khrushchev deposed
- 1968 Russian troops enter Czechoslovakia
- 1977 Brezhnev Party Secretary
- 1979 USSR occupies Afghanistan
- 1987 Party Secretary Gorbachev starts major reforms
- 1988 Troops begin to move out of Afghanistan

Africa

- 1942 Battle of El Alamein
- 1943 Allies invade North Africa
- 1948 Nationalists win power in South Africa
- 1956 Egypt nationalizes Suez Canal 'Suez Crisis'
- 1957 Ghana independent
- 1958 French settlers in Algeria revolt
- 1959 Rioting in Belgian Congo
- 1960 Sharpeville Massacre in South Africa
- 1960–3 'Wind of Change'. Independence for many African states
- 1961 Civil War in Congo UN troops move in
- 1962 Nigerian independence from France
- 1964 Mandela imprisoned for life
- 1965 White Rhodesians declare UDI
- 1967–9 Civil War in Nigeria and Biafra
- 1971 Idi Amin seizes power in Uganda Many atrocities
- 1975 Portugal gives independence to Angola and Mozambique
- 1975 Haile Selassie deposed
- 1976 Riots in Soweto, South Africa
- 1979 Tanzanian troops invade Uganda Amin deposed
- 1980 Rhodesia becomes independent as Zimbabwe
- 1981 President Sadat of Egypt assassinated
- 1986 US jets bomb Libya

Asia

- 1940 Japan occupies French Indo-China
- 1941 Japan attacks Pearl Harbor Hong Kong falls
- 1942 Japan captures Singapore, Burma, Philippines
- 1942 Battle of Midway
- 1945 Atom bombs dropped End of WORLD WAR 2
- 1947 India and Pakistan gain independence Partition riots
- 1948 Israeli independence
- 1950 China occupies Tibet
- 1950–3 Korean war
- 1954 French Indo-China independent
- 1958 'Great leap forward' in China
- 1959 Revolt in Tibet. Dalai Lama flees
- 1965 Pakistan, India clash over Kashmir
- 1966 Cultural revolution begins in China
- 1967 Six Day War. Israel defeats Arabs
- 1970 Jordan fights Palestinians
- 1971 Bangladesh War Freedom from Pakistan
- 1973 Arab-Israeli War Oil prices shoot up World economic crisis
- 1975 Khmer Rouge seize power in Cambodia. Many atrocities
- 1975 Civil War in Lebanon
- 1975 Saigon falls. Vietnam war over
- 1976 Death of Mao Tse-tung
- 1977 Army coup in Pakistan
- 1978 Vietnam invades Cambodia
- 1979 Revolution in Iran Shah deposed
- 1980 Iran/Iraq war begins
- 1982 Israel invades Lebanon
- 1982 Sri Lanka fights Tamil separatists
- 1984 Indian PM Gandhi assassinated by Sikh extremists
- 1985 Palestinian terrorists active
- 1986 President Marcos of Phillippines deposed

The Americas

- 1941 Japanese attack on Pearl Harbor Germany and Italy declare war on USA
- 1942 Battle of Midway
- 1945 Atom bombs dropped on Japan End of WORLD WAR 2
- 1946 First Session of UN
- 1946 Perón elected Argentinian President
- 1947 Truman Doctrine and Marshall Plan
- 1951 MacArthur dismissed from Korean command
- 1955 Perón exiled
- 1957 US show of strength in Lebanon
- 1959 Castro victory in Cuba
- 1960 US U2 aircraft shot down over USSR
- 1962 Independence for Jamaica and Trinidad
- 1962 Cuban missile crisis
- 1963 President John F. Kennedy assassinated
- 1963 Martin Luther King leads civil rights march
- 1965 Build up of troops in Vietnam
- 1969 Americans land on moon
- 1969 Increasing opposition to Vietnam in USA
- 1973 US signs Paris peace settlement over Vietnam
- 1973 President Allende of Chile toppled in right-wing coup. Many atrocities
- 1974 Watergate President Nixon resigns
- 1978 Camp David discussions between Israel and Egypt
- 1980 US attempt to rescue Iran hostages fails
- 1980 Civil War in El Salvador
- 1982 Argentina invades Falklands. War with UK
- 1983 US Marines invade Cuba
- 1987 Stock Market crash

Victims of the Khmer Rouge, Kampuchea (Cambodia) 1975–79

Since 1945, it is often claimed, nuclear weapons have succeeded in deterring the renewed outbreak of war. True, there has been no war in which the two super-powers have fought each other directly and no war that has spanned the globe. Whether the existence of nuclear weapons has been a significant inhibiting factor is a matter of dispute. But what cannot be disputed is that, although there has been no world war since 1945, there have been plenty of localised conflicts. The toll of human deaths alone has been at the rate of half-a-million a year on average. Add to that the misery of the wounded, the bereaved and the refugees; the destruction of property; the dislocation of economies; and the vast expenditure on weapons. The god of war has dominated the lives of hundreds of millions since 1945.

Depending on one's definition of 'war' there have been between one and two hundred during this period. One reason for such a large figure is that, with a rapidly increasing number of states, there have been a larger number of these political entities to quarrel with each other. Furthermore, the proliferation of states has coincided with a substantial increase in the lethal power of even conventional weapons. Civilians are not only considered legitimate targets in modern warfare, but they can be reached and attacked far behind 'the front line' by aerial forces. The huge casualties in the Korean, Nigerian and Vietnam conflicts were composed of substantial proportions of non-combatants.

And, of course, the more sophisticated the weapons, the more expensive they are to purchase. By the mid-1980s the world's armament's bill topped $1,000 billion p.a. 'If you want profit, prepare for war,' should be the modern amendment of the well-known saying.

☠ Countries where wars, in which at least one government was engaged, resulted in 1000 or more deaths per year. Many civilian deaths go unrecorded

The numbers indicate where there has been the greatest loss of life

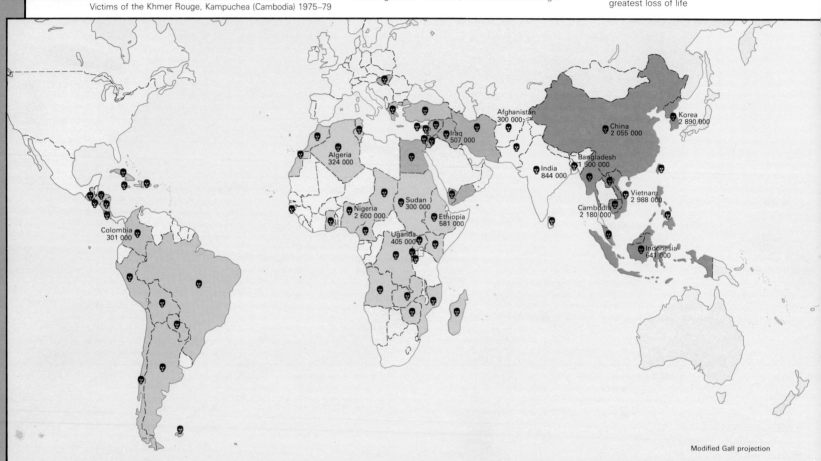

Afghanistan 300 000
Korea 2 890 000
China 2 055 000
Iraq 507 000
Algeria 324 000
Bangladesh 1 500 000
India 844 000
Vietnam 2 988 000
Nigeria 2 600 000
Sudan 300 000
Cambodia 2 180 000
Ethiopia 581 000
Uganda 405 000
Colombia 301 000
Indonesia 641 000

Modified Gall projection

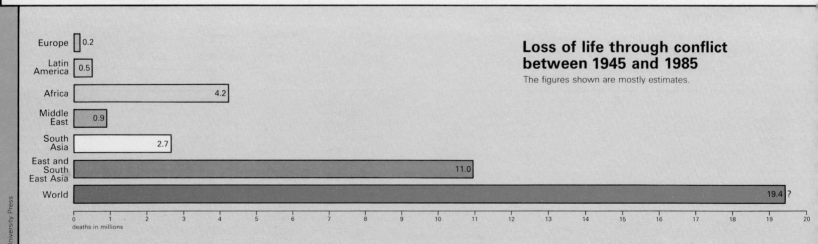

Loss of life through conflict between 1945 and 1985

The figures shown are mostly estimates.

Region	deaths in millions
Europe	0.2
Latin America	0.5
Africa	4.2
Middle East	0.9
South Asia	2.7
East and South East Asia	11.0
World	19.4 ?

deaths in millions